OLD SYNAGOGUE ESSEN —
HOUSE OF JEWISH CULTURE

THE PERMANENT EXHIBITION

KLARTEXT

Printed with the friendly help of:

 Alfried Krupp von Bohlen und Halbach-Stiftung

Imprint

City of Essen – Old Synagogue Essen, House of Jewish Culture

1st edition: september 2016

Design and Layout
Volker Pecher, Essen

Translation
Roy Kift, Essen
Franz Kubaczyk, Cologne (Article Edna Brocke)

Proof Reading
Roy Kift, Essen

Klartext Verlag, Essen

KLARTEXT

Friedrichstraße 34–38,
D-45128 Essen
Germany
info@klartext-verlag.de,
www.klartext-verlag.de

Printing and Binding:
Himmer GmbH, Druckerei und Verlag
Steinerne Furt 95
D-86167 Augsburg

ISBN 978-3-8375-1687-6
© Klartext Verlag, Essen 2016

Bibliographical information of the German Library:
The German National Library provides detailed information on the cataloguing of this title under: http://dnb.dnb.de

All rights reserved including adaptations for film, radio, CD-ROM, the translation, photocopies and extracts in reprints and usages in Germany and abroad.

Thomas Kufen
4 On this volume

Uri R. Kaufmann
5 Introduction

Peter Schwiderowski/Martina Strehlen
6 From a memorial site to a *House of Jewish Culture*

Edna Brocke
32 On commemoration and its changes in Essen and in Germany

Dorothee Rauhut
42 " ... Germany's most illustrious synagogue!" The architecture of the Old Synagogue in Essen. Reflections on the historical building

Lothar Jeromin
80 The reconstruction of the Old Synagogue, 2008–2010

Uri R. Kaufmann
122 The exhibits in the permanent exhibition

206 The authors, thanks, picture credits

On this booklet

The Old Synagogue in Essen – the House of Jewish Culture in North Rhine Westphalia – is a very special institution. It shows many facets of the culture, history and religion of the oldest non-Christian minority in Europe. There is evidence to show that Jews have lived within the borders of today's Germany since at least the 10th century. In doing so they have insisted on their right to be different. Despite the murder of millions of European Jews they have played an active part in shaping modern culture after the Second World War.

In mediaeval Europe there were Ashkenazi (Central European) Jews and Sephardic (Andalusian) Jews. And between 1730 and 1750 mystic Hasidism began to spread in the kingdom of Poland/Lithuania. Around the same time Moses Mendelssohn and a circle of scholars in Berlin began to propagate a movement for inner-Jewish Enlightenment. The three modern religious currents were created in the 1840s, and later an increasing amount of Jews regarded themselves as secular. Judaism was always diversity, a fact of which a large part of the majority society was, and still is, never aware. This is the starting point for the Old Synagogue's comprehensive programme of events, talks, concerts, readings, temporary exhibitions and "Thursday political discussions", in which you too can participate.

For many centuries there was peaceful coexistence in everyday life before the Christian church began to chafe against the presence of Jews. False accusations of child murder, well poisoning and desecration of the Eucharist were widespread in mediaeval Europe, and even continued on occasions into the 20th century. Even the Protestant reformer, Martin Luther, was the author of virulent, inflammatory, anti-Jewish statements and writings.

The aim of the Old Synagoge in Essen is not only to show diversity in contemporary Judaism, but also to demonstrate the contribution Jews are making to modern culture. Judaism has belonged to Europe for 2000 years. It has learned from discrimination to promote interreligious dialogue and make people more aware of how prejudice can arise. It is committed to using information and education to reduce anti-Jewish prejudices. The new permanent exhibition is an open invitation to us all to learn more about diversity in contemporary life, and hence about integration.

Essen, June 2016

Thomas Kufen
Lord Mayor of the city of Essen

Introduction

The Old Synagogue, consecrated in 1913, has had an unsettled history. This catalogue documents the new permanent exhibition about Jewish life around the globe today, especially the latest developments. The new permanent exhibition was opened on 10th July 2010 during the year when the city of Essen was the European Capital of Culture. Two of the staff members at the Old Synagogue, Martina Strehlen and Peter Schwiderowski, who cooperated with the former director Edna Brocke in drawing up the conception, describe how it came into being.

Dorothee Rauhut portrays the building in the context of art history and of synagogue architecture in Germany. The building made its architect, Edmund Körner, well known throughout the whole of the Ruhrgebiet.

After alterations in 1959/60 and reconstruction work in the interior of the building in 1986, a thorough overhaul became necessary when a new conception was drawn up between 2008 and 2010. The architect, Lothar Jeromin, describes the philosophy behind it and how it was turned into reality. Today the Old Synagogue, especially its interior, is one of the finest buildings in the centre of Essen.

A comprehensive article covers the exhibits in the new permanent exhibition. Alongside an introduction to synagogues all over the world, the new permanent exhibition can be divided into five sections: *Sources of Jewish Traditions, Jewish Holidays and Shabbat, Jewish Identities Today (Jewish Way of Life), History of the Jewish Community in Essen* and *History of the Building*. We also offer further historical and general notes on the exhibits. A large number of different references to specialist literature and websites offer additional material and introduce visitors to contemporary Jewish culture around the world, without forgetting local history and that of the building.

There are 23 memorial sites in North Rhine Westphalia. Prominently placed at the centre is the house of Jewish culture, the Old Synagogue in Essen. It focuses thematically on the present. Although three sections of the permanent exhibition are dedicated to the Shoah – the mass murder of European Jews – this is not all. The permanent exhibition also offers audio guides with 31 sound files in German and English, *Lehrhaus Judentum (Teaching House for Judaism)* for children and another for young people, as well as guided tours on three different themes.

In 2015 we presented almost 50 events. These included political discussions on Thursdays, lectures, readings, concerts and temporary exhibitions. We cooperate with the University of Duisburg-Essen, the Society for Christian-Jewish Cooperation in Essen, the German-French Cultural Centre, the Essen Old Synagogue Foundation, the Essen city archives, the schools department of the Evangelical church district of Essen, the Medium Forum of the Diocese of Essen and the Polish Institute Düsseldorf.

In 2015 we greeted over 33,000 guests from North Rhine Westphalia and neighbouring countries like Belgium and the Netherlands.

We hope to be able to continue our work in mediating knowledge about cultural and religious diversity. From a social and political point of view this is also necessary in the light of increasing xenophobia, a general coarsening of political culture and blatant anti-Semitism from certain sections of society.

Uri R. Kaufmann

From a memorial site to a *House of Jewish Culture*

Peter Schwiderowski/Martina Strehlen

On 14th February 2001 the *Westdeutsche Allgemeine Zeitung* (WAZ) ran a story with the following title: "The synagogue in Essen to become a Jewish Museum. A proposal by Paul Spiegel". This was the first time the general public was made aware of plans to change the concept behind the Old Synagogue, which until then had been a memorial site and a political and historical documentation forum for the city of Essen.

What the then president of the Central Council of Jews in Germany proposed had not yet been worked out in detail. Nor was there any precise idea of the future character of the building. That said, as early as 1993 the head of the Old Synagogue, Edna Brocke, had voiced some initial thoughts about redeveloping the building to a place where Jewish culture could be presented, before she even saw there was an opportunity to do so.

When the Old Synagogue was opened as an urban memorial site in November 1980 the exhibition's main theme was the Nazi history in Essen and the resistance to the regime. The former significance of the historic building as a place of Jewish cultural life played no role in this presentation. Correspondingly the memorial site was placed in rooms which, after a turbulent history and a thorough gutting of the building, in no way reminded people of the former synagogue.

It was only thanks to reconstruction work on the synagogue interior between 1986 and 1988, and the installation of a new permanent exhibition entitled *Stations of Jewish Life. From Emancipation To the Present Day* – it focused on the history of the Jewish community in Essen – that the history of the Jews and cultural aspects of Jewish life came into view.

In the early 1990s new forms of events and new contents were introduced. These were the initial attempts to set a new accent in the programme, which pointed far beyond the character of the synagogue as a memorial site. Thus the *Lehrhaus Judentum (Teaching House of Judaism)* was redeveloped to offer studies of traditional texts and the *Lehrhaus für Kinder (Teaching House for Children)* was turned into a place where young people could directly experience Jewish culture. A range of talks entitled *Thursday Conversations on Current Political Questions* began in 1994 and this established the Old Synagogue as a forum for critical political discussions. In addition, age-specific educational programmes in the form of *Lehrhäuser für Jugendliche (Teaching Houses for Youth)* were introduced to make people more aware of political aspects in their lives.

The uncompleted Essen synagogue, ca. 1914

8 From a memorial site to a *House of Jewish Culture*

The former synagogue – a cultural monument

At the time it was opened the synagogue in Essen was one of the finest examples of synagogue architecture in Germany. It could hold around 1,400 visitors and was even one of the largest freestanding synagogues north of the Alps. The fact that its exterior had survived almost undamaged during the Second World War made the building one of the most important monuments to Jewish culture in Germany.

Nonetheless the outstanding architectural quality of the building was ignored for more than four decades after the Second World War. It was used solely for installing exhibitions, a clear expression that no regard whatsoever was paid to its architectural design. Meanwhile, in the 1990s, people in the Old Synagogue, and a few other interested parties outside the building, slowly became aware of the potential of the site.

In addition the large public response to programmes like those offered by the Teaching Houses, showed that visitors were not only interested in Jewish culture in general, but also in themes that went beyond the persecution during the Nazi era.

Thus when the President of the Central Council of Jews in Germany, Paul Spiegel, put forward his public proposals in 2001 he was able to link this with the transformation in public interest and perceptions. Happily, the then Minister-President of the Federal State of North Rhine-Westphalia (NRW), Wolfgang Clement, took up Spiegel's initiative and asked for more information on ideas and potentials during a visit to the site on 23rd May. Subsequently a steering group was set up, that met for the first time on 20th June 2001. It consisted of representatives of the NRW government, the city of Essen and the Central Council of Jews in Germany. They were given the job of preparing the project in terms of content, programme, finances and organisation.

At first they agreed not to plan the future Old Synagogue in the form of a Jewish Museum. Thus they set the course for the building to become what was later called a *House of Jewish Culture;* i.e. the main accent was to be on presenting a lively cultural and learning space rather than a museum dealing with the past.

On 26th October 2001 a hearing took place in the Old Synagogue, in which twelve academic experts from home and abroad participated. They included representatives of Jewish and other museums, academic institutes, art historians, Judaists, architects and cultural educationalists. This mixture of professions reflected the complex task of reshaping the building to meet the new aims. Hence the main debates were concerned with the architecture of the building,

Jewish culture and educational questions. The hearing helped people to carve out the issues and highlight possible future action.

In the following year a feasibility study was published that, for the first time, set out more precise aims with reference to the spatial potentials of the building. One of its themes was the access to the building: here it proposed a new variation, an open stairway (this was later turned into reality in a similar form). The study also suggested that a new generous exhibition space should be created on the bottom floor so as to leave the main room beneath the dome free for events. This idea was later changed in favour of a solution comprising a blend of the space with exhibition areas.

The feasibility study also included the former Rabbi's house, directly adjacent to the synagogue. Sadly it was excluded in later plans for the *House of Jewish Culture*. Since May 2011 it has housed a number of academic institutes. These include the Salomon Ludwig Steinheim Institute for German-Jewish History at the University of Duisburg-Essen.

The next important stage in development was a design competition between 2005 and 2006. Organised by the real estate department of the city of Essen, it was launched in autumn 2005. It was open to applicants throughout Europe but the number of participants was restricted to 12 teams. Precisely because the tasks involved required multidisciplinary skills, the teams were made up of architects, exhibition makers, lighting designers and media experts.

The aim was formulated as follows in the call for tender: "In future the Old Synagogue will be continuing to emphasise the themes mentioned above, but they will be deepened by including the building itself to enable visitors to encounter Judaism. The heart of the programme will have nothing to do with the past, looking backwards, or historical factors. However, since tradition and history are the keys to understanding Judaism today, history – in this sense – also has its place. That said, the central point of emphasis will be placed on encountering a living culture featuring both traditional and modern ways of life."

The request was for creative outlines that had not yet reached a detailed planning stage, but would nonetheless serve as a starting point for concrete implementation. The jury met on 3rd March 2006 and awarded three prizes and one accolade. The first prize went to a team entitled space4/luna.licht-architektur/jangled nerves in Stuttgart. Its design focused consistently on the principles behind the original designs. It retained the axial nature and symmetry of the building and pleaded for an opening of the fourth original stairwell. The main room was planned to be a central meeting place, as it is indeed today. Another proposal that was also realised was to move the administration from the upper floor to the base level. This would create a new exhibition area, which now presents the central section on *Jewish Way of Life*.

Two further levels, above the Torah shrine, could also be gained for extra exhibition areas. They now contain sections on the *History of the Building* and, in the mezzanine, the *History of the Jewish Community*.

The award-winning ceremony for the design competition, 23rd March 2006

Although there was now a plan envisioning the design of the new *House of Jewish Culture*, there was still no funding. The projected costs were reckoned to be in the area of 7,400,000 Euros. These included money to redesign the area around the synagogue. For it very quickly became clear that an attractive *House of Jewish Culture* had to highlight its external features. Furthermore such a project would also be an opportunity for the synagogue to considerably improve its original quality, if not to the extent of attaining its original scale of magnificence. This meant particularly the space between the Old Synagogue, the Centennial Fountain and the Old Catholic Church of Peace.

Almost two years after the end of the competition the overall funding was finally established. 80% of funds would be provided by the Federal State of North Rhine-Westphalia as part of its urban promotion programme. The remainder would be provided by twelve other fund-giving bodies, both private and public, and by many other small donations.

On 27th February 2008 the council of the city of Essen voted in favour of the new plans to combine work on the synagogue building with work on the exhibition areas. The first measures went into operation in September 2008. Within the space of less than two years a huge number of architectural changes to the interior and exterior of the building were created, including five new exhibition areas. A sixth exhibition area, in the entrance to the main room, was added somewhat later.

The Idea and Concept behind the *House of Jewish Culture*

Diversity beneath a single roof

It is quite common for exhibition makers to come up against a situation where an existing building or a newly-built building has to accommodate a new exhibition. In this case the location provides a space and a roof for the presentation, and the presentation is at the centre of the programme.

As already mentioned, for many years the Old Synagogue building was merely a hollow shell in which to present exhibitions of past history. The sole exception in relationship to the synagogue itself was a theme on its desecration in 1938. Beyond that, however, the original significance of the building was almost completely ignored. It needed a long process of development before people began to become more aware of this dimension.

This was precisely where the new concept for the Old Synagogue as a *House of Jewish Culture* began. To some extent the new design and concept would give visitors the opportunity to undergo a lengthy path of discovery. Taken together, the building itself, the exhibition areas and the many different events would make up the *House of Jewish Culture*.

Culture and history, political discussions and educational work, architecture and aesthetics, philosophy and current encounters should all have a place here. Hence it is no surprise that the final image of the Old Synagogue was intended to be somewhat nebulous: a mixture of a museum, a memorial site, a cultural centre and a place of experience. Today all these functions continue to exist alongside one another.

Opening up fresh perspectives

Two main types of institution are responsible for introducing Judaism to a wider public in Germany: memorial sites and Jewish museums. Memorial sites often confine our current encounters with Judaism to the period under the Nazis, persecution and the Shoah. They concentrate on history and politics. By contrast, Jewish museums not only deal with historical aspects but mainly focus on religious rituals.

The focus on the Shoah can make the Jews seem almost exclusively a group of victims. Such an outlook mostly evokes dismay and grief. Against this background non-Jews often feel tense and insecure when confronted with Jewish themes. A further problem is that they tend to view Judaism mainly as something to do with the past.

A concentration on religious rituals gives the impression that Jewish culture is religion; and that to be a Jew is to be part of a community of believers like Christianity or Islam. Such a blinkered view does not do justice to Jews' own image of themselves and their uniqueness.

A *House of Jewish Culture* indicates that another starting point has been selected. This enables visitors to have a new, broader perspective, and to at least question the validity of clichés and fixed ideas. The main thing is to foster people's curiosity and their desire to find out more about a broadly unknown, vital and diverse culture. Within this framework other themes like history, persecution and destruction can also be introduced, although these are only secondary.

In order to enable people to have a broader view of Jews as being far more than simply a religious community, the *House of Jewish Culture* should also deal with Jewish identities, life styles and areas of everyday life. The very title of the innovative exhibition area, *Jewish Way of Life*, indicates what this is all about.

The building tells its story

Anyone who looks at the former synagogue and learns that the exterior has remained almost completely in its original state whilst the interior consists solely of reconstructions is almost bound to start asking questions about the designer and the building's turbulent history. The building tells its own story. It is the first perceptible exhibit in the overall presentation. The building is a symbol of Jewish culture in general and was a centre of Jewish life for twenty-five years. In particular it is a symbol of the self-confidence of German Judaism.

The former synagogue, now the Haus Industrieform (House of Industrial Design), with the memorial sarcophagus, ca. 1961

The House of Industrial Design, main entrance, 1961

But the history of the building also bears witness to the way it has been dealt with by non-Jewish society after the Second World War. For around fifteen years after 1945 the interior of the damaged building stood almost untouched on the edge of the inner city area. In 1949 a sarcophagus was erected on the stairway leading up to the main entrance, as a memorial to the Jewish citizens of Essen who had been murdered by the Nazis.

After the city bought up the synagogue in 1959 – in the same year the Jewish community in Essen built a new synagogue elsewhere from the proceeds – it began comprehensive building measures in the interior of the building, during which all remaining furnishings were lost. In accordance with the dynamics of the German economic miracle an industrial design museum was set up inside the old synagogue in 1961.

The House of Industrial Design, the gutted, converted main room. South-west view, 1964

The setting up of the Old Synagogue memorial site in 1980 marked an important new step in the history of its usage. Initially the memorial site was devoted almost exclusively to the history of National Socialism, persecution and resistance to dictatorship. But very gradually people began to think more about the former Jewish significance of the place and how to include this also as a theme.

Given this fact it was clear that the building was a significant exhibit in itself, that could lead visitors to ask questions about Judaism in general and the attitudes and self-image of the non-Jewish majority society. These questions were taken up and dealt with in depth in the exhibition areas.

The exhibition

After the conversion of the Old Synagogue and its new concept as a *House of Jewish Culture*, a new permanent exhibition was opened, comprising several different thematic areas: *History of the Building, History of the Jewish Community in Essen, The Synagogue, Sources of Jewish Traditions, Jewish Holidays* and *Jewish Way of Life*.

The different exhibition areas are spread over various levels in the building. They are not only self enclosed but also independent of one another.

Two areas, *History of the Building* and *History of the Jewish Community in Essen,* deal with themes connected with history, the city of Essen and the synagogue building. Hence they tell of the turbulent history of the building – the main exhibit – and the people who founded it. The other exhibition areas deal with cultural and religious matters. Here the themes and exhibits presented in *Sources of Jewish Traditions, Jewish Holidays* and *the Synagogue* may be considered as thoroughly "classic" for a Jewish museum and, as such something that you would expect from an exhibition on Judaism. That said, the form of presentation is unusual. Alongside modern exhibits great value is laid on the use of media and modern installations. There again, the *Jewish Way of Life* may be regarded as a completely new approach to presenting Jewish culture.

The lack of a recommended route through the building is part of the overall concept. All exhibition areas can be visited in any sequence you like. Thus visitors are free to decide which, and how many, exhibition areas to view.

The exhibition areas
History of the Building

Since the huge domed building was opened as a synagogue on 25th September 1913 it has experienced a turbulent history. This ranges from the final years of the Wilhelmine Empire via the Weimar Republic and the National Socialist regime, all the way to the Federal Republic of Germany.

The building was used as a synagogue, and hence as a centre of local Jewish life, for only the first twenty-five years of its existence until 1938. After this it was subjected to acts of destruction and architectural changes. These can also be interpreted in terms of the attitudes of the non-Jewish majority society to Jewish culture and their way of dealing with a cultural monument.

The exhibition area entitled *History of the Building* uses old photos and original exhibits to tell of the changes made to the Old Synagogue. Here an information terminal – computer screens with a huge number of images and written documents – invites visitors to approach the theme in a more systematic manner.

History of the Building area, 2010

History of the Jewish Community in Essen

The first mention of Jews in Essen dates back to a document written in 1291. That said, it is only really possible to speak of a significant Jewish community in the city during the era of industrialisation at the end of the 19th century. In 1933 it comprised around 5,000 members, who actively contributed to Essen's cultural, social and economic life. Around 2,500 Jewish citizens in Essen were murdered during the Shoah. Others survived by fleeing the country and emigrating.

After the Second World War the arduous task of rebuilding a new Jewish community, consisting mainly of Eastern European refugees, no longer took place in the damaged old synagogue but in the adjacent former Rabbi's house. In 1959 the Jewish community moved into a new synagogue in Sedanstraße. This has since been the centre of practising Jews in Essen. The former synagogue and the Rabbi's house were purchased by the local authority.

History of the Jewish Community in Essen area, 2010

The exhibition area entitled *History of the Jewish Community in Essen* informs visitors about Jewish life in the city. It mainly focuses on the first half of the twentieth century. Personal objects like poetry albums, photos, emigration diaries, school reports, documents and medals awarded to Jewish citizens of Essen (also in the countries to which they emigrated), all have their own moving history. Here particular attention is devoted to the family of Rabbi Samuel.

There is also a reading corner containing publications from the first decades of the twentieth century. An installation with computer screens containing a huge number of documents allows visitors to systematically explore Jewish life in Essen.

Ten synagogues in the entrance area, with a wooden model of the Essen synagogue, 2011

The Synagogue

In the Diaspora the synagogue is the centre of Jewish life and culture. By contrast with a Christian church it is not a sacred place, for it only needs the presence of a Torah scroll to turn a room into a synagogue.

The exhibition area entitled *The Synagogue* deals with the history and features of synagogues all over the world. Photos reveal common features and the conditions necessary for a building to be regarded as a synagogue. There are strong regional differences in the architecture and within the buildings themselves. Here it is clear that each synagogue has been influenced by the culture of its particular country.

That said, there are also differences depending on religious points of view, or the origins of specific Jewish communities. Large format photos and a wooden model of the interior of the synagogue in Essen reveal the features of liberal attitudes and a religious philosophy which arose in the German Reich during the 19th century. By contrast, another wooden model shows the synagogue in Halberstadt as an example of an orthodox community. In this way it is easy to distinguish the different approaches in liberal and orthodox synagogues.

Jewish Holidays area in the north gallery. In the foreground the Hanukkah glass case, 2011

Sources of Jewish Traditions

A basic element of every culture is the upkeep of traditions. The exhibition area entitled *Sources of Jewish Traditions* gives an insight into some of the traditions of this culture which goes back more than 5000 years.

The history of Jewish traditions since the creation of the world can be interpreted as the defining source of Jewish identity. Hence the south wall of the room is covered by a large chronological display of selected events from Jewish and non-Jewish history. An installation containing the names and pictures of Jewish personalities throughout history indicates the links between the various generations.

The Torah, a traditional text, and other objects of religious and cultural practice, symbolise Jewish religion. The central rites of the cycle of life – birth, Bar-/Bat-Mitzvah (maturity), marriage and death – are defining dates in a person's life.

Finally the Jewish calendar serves as a general framework for Jews all over the world. An impressive installation, featuring two large gear wheels on the north wall of the room shows the synchronisation between the Jewish and the Gregorian calendar.

Jewish Holidays

Holidays are important anchor points in the Jewish annual calendar. Many are connected to agricultural aspects in Israel, thereby expressing the particular bond with this country.

Jewish holidays are a reminder of significant dates in the history of the Jewish people for they preserve collective experiences and personal images. The great significance given to them was originally recorded in the Essen synagogue in six stained-glass windows dedicated to the six main Jewish holidays and standing above the women's gallery. It was impossible to reconstruct them after they were destroyed during the night of the 1938 pogrom.

The exhibition area entitled *Jewish Holidays* uses ritual and everyday objects to present the well-known holidays. Alongside the six main holidays, that were originally portrayed in the windows and mentioned in the Torah, there are two additional holidays which later arose, each of which is well known and highly popular.

The glass cases contain only a few highly valuable, precious ritual objects. The majority of the exhibits are colourful, modern, sometimes kitschy examples of Judaica, and everyday objects made of plastic or plush. This shows that children are not only passive participants in the holidays, but also take over some of the tasks themselves on many occasions.

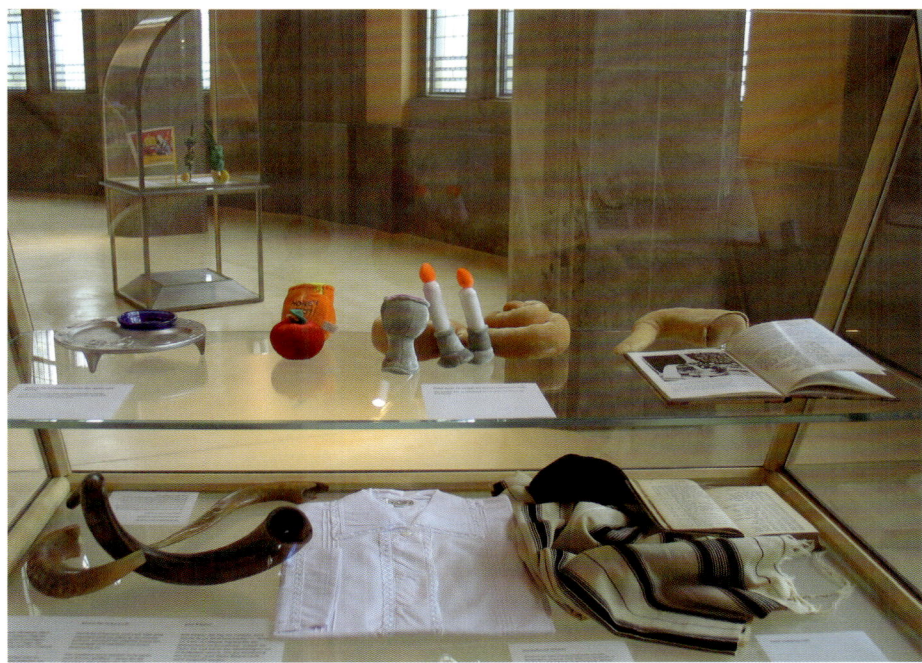

Glass case with exhibits on the two major holidays, Rosh ha-Shanah (New Year) and Yom Kippur (Day of Repentance), 2010

Jewish Way of Life

Contrary to widespread opinion Judaism is much more than a religion and cannot be summed up in the term "religious community". It is an all embracing living culture that simultaneously contains diversity, differences and similarities alike. Above all Judaism does not fit in with many existing clichés.

The exhibition area entitled *Jewish Way of Life* invites visitors to enjoy some unusual aspects of Jewish life, and get an insight into how this way of life is shown in music, video clips and films, in dance, language and clothing, in social and sporting organisations, in newspapers and periodicals. These are only a few of the areas treated with humour and surprising facts.

Jewish Way of Life area. Interactive station showing Israeli folk dances, 2010

Jewish Way of Life area. The "dietary" glass case. In the background the glass case with clothing, 2010

Jewish Way of Life area. The interactive multi-touch table featuring major Jewish communities, 2010

Old Synagogue Essen – House of Jewish Culture

A lively cultural venue

The exhibition areas that do not primarily deal with historical themes show Judaism as a modern, lively and diverse culture. Unusual exhibits, interactive stations and a widespread use of media ensure that children and young people, who make up a particularly high proportion of visitors, can be reached.

Here you can not only learn dance and listen to Israeli pop music, but also find out more about kosher diets and the Hebrew language. Interactive maps of various large Jewish cities show you where you can find a synagogue, kosher bakery or a Jewish bikers' meeting point.

Particularly in the *Jewish Way of Life,* but also in the other exhibition areas, the selection of modern exhibits and mediation methods help to do away with the cliché of Judaism as a culture and religion of the past.

Equally the Jewish pre-war community, the synagogue founders and memories of the murdered Jews also have their place within the building. The life and merits of Jewish citizens in and around Essen are thematised along with their fate during the Nazi dictatorship. Information terminals in the exhibition areas entitled *History of the Jewish Community in Essen* and *History of the Building* enable visitors to delve into history themselves.

Since the Old Synagogue is an official urban memorial site, the city of Essen and the Jewish community in Essen jointly stage an event on 9th November every year to commemorate the pogrom in 1938.

Furthermore the main room contains a remembrance book for the Jewish citizens in Essen who were murdered. This book is part of a remembrance book project initiated by the Old Synagogue. The project once gave interested people and groups like school classes the opportunity to write a biography of a person who was murdered. To help them the Old Synagogue put biographic material at their disposal, mediated contacts with relatives and friends and, where necessary, provided help in composing the text.

Much consideration has been given to ensure that the various exhibition sections fit well into all the different spaces in order to allow visitors to experience the impressive main room from all perspectives. The sections are generously spaced out to avoid giving an impression of restriction. It was an important aim to preserve the impressive feeling of space, despite the many glass cases and installations.

The exhibition is consciously planned so that it can include new aspects on special occasions. Educational programmes enhance the exhibition. Here the newly conceived Teaching House for Children deserves a special mention because it covers all the themes in the exhibition.

Alongside information on Jewish history and culture a lively cultural life also has its place in the Old Synagogue. A huge programme catering for different interests and ages show the diversity of Jewish culture.

The choir of the University of Essen performing the oratorio "Annelies" by James Whitbourn in the Old Synagogue, 1st February 2016

Concerts featuring religious, traditional and modern Jewish music are amongst the most popular events. To give but one example, in February 2015 the Essen University choir presented a highly successful performance of the oratorio "Annelies" by James Whitbourn.

But concerts with no reference to Jewish life also attract a huge number of visitors on account of the impressive building and its acoustics.

Besides this, there are talks, podium discussions and readings on various themes. Since 1994 a highly regarded monthly (apart from in the holidays) series of *Thursday Conversations on Politics, Culture and Society,* has greatly enriched the political culture of the city. Other lectures and lecture series deal with subjects like Jewish life in Europe.

There are not only events for adults but also for children and young people. Thus pupils from Cologne presented a highly successful performance of a Purim musical entitled "Megille Reloaded" during the NRW Jewish Culture Days in 2011.

One particularly important pillar of the work with children is the above-mentioned Teaching House for Children, that was conceived to fit in with the

Old Synagogue Essen – House of Jewish Culture   25

new exhibition. It has been a part of the synagogue programme since autumn 2011. It is addressed to primary-school children but can also be adapted, where necessary, for other age groups. Here the children learn a few basic concepts about Judaism in a light-hearted manner; the main emphasis lies not so much in the cognitive area as in the highly playful elements. Teachers and educationalists can choose from a huge number of modules in advance. There are modules on Jewish holidays, Jewish traditions and Jewish history, all of which have connections to the building or the exhibition.

For example children can discover what a synagogue is, decorate a Sukkah (a temporary hut) for Sukkoth (the Feast of Tabernacles), or find out more about the life of a woman called Doris Moses who was only eleven when the synagogue was desecrated on the night of the 9/10th November 1938. The following day she climbed through one of the broken windows in the synagogue in order to collect a few scattered remains and mosaic stones from the rubble around the destroyed Torah shrine. In 1988 she returned to Essen after many years, to donate the stones to the exhibition in the Old Synagogue.

In addition children can get to know more about the dishes prepared for the Seder meal that marks the start of the Pessach festivities, or learn Israeli folk dances. Every module in the Teaching House contains games and tasks that enable the children to explore the Old Synagogue. After such positive experiences the children are only too keen to return to the building when they are older and studying subjects like religion or the history of Judaism.

For young people between the ages of thirteen and eighteen there are workshops on the *History of the Synagogue Building* and *Jewish Holidays*. The workshops work with a huge variety of methods. Alongside interactive elements from theatre-in-education, texts and research material are also used. The rooms in the Old Synagogue and the permanent exhibition are integrated into the workshops to enable the young people to experience them more vividly. Thus young people can become acquainted with the Old Synagogue not only as a place full of history, but also as a lively cultural venue where the past meets the present.

More programmes for young people and adults will be developed in the coming years. These will include guided tours on special themes, information and further-education events, as well as source booklets and brochures on historic and religious themes.

The Old Synagogue and the new Edmund-Körner-Platz, 2010

An open, inviting building

Alongside special exhibition presentations, the interior design of the Old Synagogue and its exterior areas are at the centre of the conception for the *House of Jewish Culture*. Here form and content are matched in a very particular way.

In doing so, a further reconstruction of the historic details in the main room of the former synagogue and in the area of the former forecourt has been consciously excluded. Such a reconstruction would anyway be impossible in the main room since no old photos can give reliable information about the original colouring of the interior and its special atmosphere at that time.

It is much more essential to look at the current programme of the house which concentrates on the present and future. A backward-looking historical approach would have contradicted this.

In this respect work began on designing an open inviting exterior area in front of the former synagogue. As mentioned above, in 1949 a sarcophagus to commemorate the murder of the Jews in Essen was placed on a cross-facing plinth on the steps leading up to the synagogue entrance. This stone sarcophagus in a prominent place was an expression of the contents within the building.

The main room of the Old Synagogue with a view of the Torah Ark, 2010

In the new conception the first action to be taken was to remove the plinth. The sarcophagus was then moved to the former Rabbi's garden as an exhibit of the building's architectural history after 1945, where it has become a part of the exhibition presentation. The current design of the steps leading up to the main entrance has a spacious feel. Even more space was gained by the removal of a single lane of traffic in front of the steps. The newly created Edmund Körner square stretches between the synagogue, the Centennial Fountain and the Old Catholic Church of Peace. It not only offers people a space to rest awhile, but has also raised the quality of the urban surroundings.

A second accent was set in the decision about what colours the main room should have. The partial conversions that took place between 1986 and 1988 emphasised the "remembrance" character of the building. Architectural losses during the 1938 November pogrom were specially marked out. Blank circular areas were intended to indicate the places where mosaics were once placed. The overall colouring was rather cold and its sobriety underlined the "memorial" atmosphere in the room. Now the large areas of walls were given a warm apricot colour, whereas the underside of the dome was set off in lilac.

View from the organ gallery to the main room, looking west, 2010

A third accent was set by opening up the interior to make it an inviting place to pause and reflect. Three areas – on the former organ gallery above the Torah shrine in the east, somewhat above the gallery in the west and higher up on the mezzanine – are now included in the tour of the building. They were not previously accessible to the general public.

The gallery, which was previously surrounded by a raised walkway in the area of the six main windows, now stretches generously over the whole area right up to the windows, leaving an unimpeded view of the main room.

A new lighting concept played a decisive role in opening up the space. During the reconstruction that took place between 1986 and 1988 a decision was made to have a huge representative chandelier hanging over the centre of the room from a large amount of rods placed at the height of the gallery. This "forest" of rods attached to the ceiling beneath the dome not only disturbed the atmosphere on the ground floor but also considerably impeded the view from the gallery above. The chandelier was done away with and its understated replacement now enables visitors to experience the room in all its depth and openness.

Rest area in the mezzanine with view of the main room, 2011

30   From a memorial site to a *House of Jewish Culture*

Benches, chairs, loungers and seats now await visitors on all levels of the building from the ground floor to the mezzanine: all of them allow hitherto unknown perspectives of the space.

The main aim behind the concept of a *House of Jewish Culture* was to upgrade the urban quality of the surrounding area and the quality of time spent within the building. Together, the contents and the aesthetic interior design have now created a framework for an inviting and open *House of Jewish Culture*.

The Old Synagogue – a House of Jewish Culture and a venue for urban society

Anyone with any idea of the turbulent usage history of the former synagogue, will perhaps understand why the institution intends to retain its diverse programme in the future; why the building regards itself as being open to urban society as a whole and why the city of Essen regards it as its duty to support the building as part of its overall social responsibility.

However this also means that the Old Synagogue – *the House of Jewish Culture* – will no more become a place for the Jewish community to gather to pray. There are other places where Jewish citizens can practice their religion, for example the synagogue belonging to the Jewish community in Essen. The dividing line between providing information about the many sides of Jewish culture and upholding everyday Jewish practices is not simply a formal consideration but underlines the innovative concept now in place in the Old Synagogue.

From time to time there is pious talk about people "wanting to heal" the fragile history of the site by making it a "sacred" place once more. Such a wish is expressed in a desire to hand over a part of the newly designed house to the Jewish community (at least on a temporary basis), in order to link it with the time when it was indeed a practising synagogue. Apart from the fact that such a decision would put in question the open character of the institution, we must also consider another basic factor.

After the Second World War many decades went by before the members of the majority non-Jewish society in the city were finally prepared to face the destruction and desecration of the building and ask themselves hard questions about what had happened. Thus the former synagogue has become a part of the painful conflicts and customs that have occurred in the cultural life of Essen and its history. It is now a place which encourages people to become more politically sensitive.

The orientation of the new concept towards the present and future underlines the fact that here history should not be "consigned to the dustbin" in a rigid ritual of memories and remembrance. On the contrary: it emphasises the lasting responsibility placed on the urban society to guarantee the retention of a lively cultural centre in the heart of the city.

.

On commemoration and its changes in Essen and in Germany

Edna Brocke

Any attempt to construct a narrative of a "collective" past aims to form a consensus on the origins of the present and the duties that these origins result in. In the Federal Republic of Germany, the process of coming to terms with the past ("Vergangenheitsbewältigung") has always been based on two pillars: the belief in the power of "enlightenment", which could prevent history from repeating itself, and an attitude of humility through remembrance and reappraisal as a way to "heal" and reconcile (also and especially) with regards to the victims of the Shoah.

In this context, numerous memorials have been built all over Germany and given a central role in this process. The use of the Old Synagogue as a memorial must also be seen as part of this larger picture.

Is collective remembrance possible?

One of the leitmotifs of most memorials and their educational programmes was – and in part still is –"Never again war. Never again Auschwitz."

Despite legitimate doubts as to whether we can "learn from history" at all, this ostensibly plausible two-part sentence has led to completely opposite conclusions, based on the different experiences had during the 20th century.
- Some say "never again" and mean their own history and that of their forefathers: Never again shall Germany start a war.
- Most Jews and almost certainly most Jewish Israelis say "never again" and mean: never again shall we, without a fight, let ourselves become victims.

Those on one side (maybe?) have learned from World War Two, the others from the Shoah.

The dominance of historical science

For a long period, historical science has claimed to "objectively" examine, categorise and assess the object of its research. It seems to me as if this self-perception has often lead to a de-objectification of the object. In the Old Synagogue, too, Jews for a long time only became subjects during the annual programme of visits for Jewish visitors who formerly lived in Essen. Other than that, historical science seemed to show more interest in dead Jews or "victims". Around the turn of the millennium, the historians' monopolised interpretation was questioned for the first time. One of the reasons for this was the late unveiling of the role that historical science played during the Nazi regime. It wasn't until the German Historians Day 1999, that it became clear that this was also, and especially, an issue of criticism among historians themselves and that living Judaism had not been seriously considered before.[1] The difficulties historians had with such a restricted role are also highlighted in a comment by Reinhart Koselleck:

"This forced selection is dangerous because every act of display means also concealment. Showing means hiding. Actually," to quote Ranke, "everything might have been completely different from what was shown so far. That is why our second creed as historians is to pay attention to the hidden, the invisible, to the things behind and between people and their events. These are, however, the continuously repeated or only slowly changing conditions of any event. From a scientific point of view, it's the repetitive structures that permeate into all events, causing them and making them possible. [...] His text might not be scientifically refutable, but it can always be overhauled. For a historian, writing his or her last sentence never means having spoken the final word on an issue."[2]

During the 1990s and 2000s, it was therefore mostly historians who repeatedly talked about and criticised what they saw as a "ritualised remembrance", while at the same time overlooking their own role in the reappraisal of German history.

No "collective" remembering, but a "collective" commemoration?

At the same time, both politicians and other members of the 'majority society' felt that their own expectations, wishes and needs for commemoration were incompatible with those of the Jewish minority (Jewish communities, Jews who are not part of a community). The inherent and objective dilemma could often be felt. It was exactly these suspicions that were repressed by creating the – undoubtedly correct but still not completely accurate – pair of terms "perpetrator/victim". Inviting historians as keynote speakers to commemoration ceremonies for many years (also in the Old Synagogue), for example on the 9th of November, has cemented this inadequate double term. The hope was to bridge this gap by hosting these commemorative events together with the local Jewish community which, for reasons of Jewish commemorative tradition, often added a Jewish liturgical supplement to the historian's speech. Although it was often quite obvious that the two groups were trying to accomplish something that only made them confront their own foreignness vis-a-vis each other, the wish for a "collective commemoration" – influenced by Christian theological thinking – prevailed.[3]

Ulrike Jureit rightfully pointed out the main differences that remind us of the structural problems of "collective commemoration": "We therefore have to understand what religious recollection means in contrast to historical recollection and what the religious promise of redemption is based on."[4] She refers to the quotation from a speech by German Federal President Richard von Weizsäcker in 1988: "The secret of redemption is remembering." This long standing Jewish tradition up to the Enlightenment, over the centuries aided the development of a specific Jewish tradition in relation to commemoration. This article aims to also keep this tradition in mind.

The Old Synagogue as a memorial site

When I was asked in 1987 by the then Head of Cultural Affairs whether I was ready to become the director of the Old Synagogue Essen, I asked for some time to think it over since, at that time, the majority society was mainly focussed on the restoration of their own shattered collective identity. Many tried to do so using the few shining examples of resistance. There was both a lack of political acceptance and empathic capacity to see the fate of the different groups of victims.[5]

When the Old Synagogue was turned into a memorial site in 1980, control of the house was therefore taken by members of the Association of Victims of the Nazi Regime (VVN)[6] who then used it to present their first and only permanent exhibition "Resistance and persecution in Essen 1933–1945".[7]

When I took over my position in January 1988, I knew that this permanent exhibition – as defined by the house – would have to be displayed at a different location in Essen and that the former Synagogue needed a completely different permanent exhibition: one, that would deal with Jewish history, Jewish life and the Jewish founders of this house.

The responsible politicians, however, were not yet ready for such a reorientation. The compromise was to move the existing "resistance exhibition" to the south section of the women's gallery while an additional exhibition on Jewish history would be developed and displayed in the main room. This exhibition, however, had also been developed by a historian prior to my inauguration. Since the exhibition was scheduled to open ten months later, most of my objections on the matter as an expert on Judaism went unheard. "Stages in a Jewish life. From

Jewish emancipation to the present" was opened on 5 November 1988 and was shown until 2008. The failure to view Jewish history as an individual topic (instead of only being seen in the context of the Nazi period) as well as Jewish thinking, life and commemoration, was not limited to Essen or the Old Synagogue. In truth, this attitude was characteristic of large parts of even those academic and political circles that had tried throughout the 1970s to carefully approach the topic of national socialism. The next step was made in 1998 by establishing the Old Synagogue Foundation. Responsible for its development and its official permit was the then head of the Chamber of Industry and Commerce (IHK). Some of the foundation's members saw the need to rethink the traditional German ideas and activities associated with a "memorial site" at a location such as a former Synagogue, especially such an impressive one in the heart of a major city. They also realised that this particular place could not be part of the usual, and at that time preferred, attempt to combine the evaluation of events and deeds during the Nazi regime.

They also supported the wish that a memorial at this location must implicitly recognise the bigger political picture, as its work up to that point had only focussed on historical matters. This solely historical perspective, by its very nature, obstructed the view of the coming socio-political processes. Especially because the Jewish people throughout their history – as a minority – actively strived to acculturate to the majority society[8] without giving up their cultural independence, the inclusion of their view into the work at the Old Synagogue was of special importance. In this regard, I had already – following the EU Summit in Essen in 1994 – established the discussion round "Thursday Talk – on Politics, Culture, Society". Its objective was to take a look at political processes beyond local political discussions in Essen and, if necessary, to analyse them in a timely manner. In other words: to re-focus on the wider community.

The Old Synagogue as a "location"

The original role of this location – which was turned into a memorial site after 1945 –, its geographic position and its acceptance in the population, were not part of the reflections prior to its establishment as an institution in 1980. It makes a significant difference whether a future memorial site was a former concentration camp, a former labour camp, a former torture chamber at a police station or a former synagogue.

But since it was the majority society's wish when establishing memorial sites to find ways to continue to live with their own history – however this was cobbled together –, Jews have been reduced to the role of victims and thus objects of their own political and historical interests.[9] The Jews themselves were rarely given an independent voice in the exhibitions and concepts.

It is not the intention here to advocate a kind of topolatry[10], but it is a simple insight that the site of a memorial influences the type of work that can and must be done there. A memorial site at a place of horror will necessarily have to focus on different things to one, for example, set in a former synagogue – even if in both cases the responsibility for the site lies with the majority society. This aspect had to be taken into account in a new concept that would bring together both location and content.

Place of memory with a Jewish note

It is not only the location that matters but also the discourse on what the terms memory, remembrance, commemoration etc. mean and what part of these we want to release into the public sphere. This is especially true in light of the fact that the non-Jewish majority needs to remember in a completely different way to a Jewish one – and vice versa. Memories are an early stage of remembrance because memory material only turns into true memory and remembrance through analysis, editing and repetition. This view should form the underlying concept for the remembrance work at the Old Synagogue Essen. That is why remembering or commemorating has different connotations for Jews and non-Jews. "To be able to link images and events to memories, we need more than the image fragments stored in our brains – we need the ability to remember. If this ability withers, we not only loose the feeling of identity, but also of community: since our memories can only be fragmented and personal, we need to reconstruct them together with other people who can add to them, correct and accentuate them. The result of this process is a vivid, interesting and true image of ourselves. And only through collectively remembering will we become part of one another. The strongest bond between people is the bond of a collective past. To be able to tell our own story, we therefore need co-authors."[11]

According to Aleida Assmann, in this context, "anniversaries (are) such important interfaces between individual and collective memory."[12]

Since memories can only be analysed and edited in juxtaposition to their counterpart, oblivion, every work of remembrance includes a deep dialectical tension – a tension that we must both endure and shape.

"Any search in the Hebrew Bible for the value of oblivion will be in vain. It only knows the horror of oblivion. Oblivion, the opposite of memory, has a completely negative connotation throughout this scripture. It is the cardinal sin – the root of all other sins."[13]

Yosef Hayim Yerushalmi has thoroughly analysed the complex relationship between history, in terms of 'objective' facts, and memory, in terms of 'subjective' individual and collective interpretations of historical events, with regard to the Jewish understanding of history and the Shoah.[14]

Even the term 'objective' historiography is problematic because the issue of objectivity is particularly disputed among historians. A Catholic religious education specialist provided the following comment on this matter: "Amidst the general 'remembrance boom' of recent years, the book sketches us the outlines of a 'culture of remembrance'. ... For a 'culture of remembrance' is more an ideal than a reality in our society. It means an honest examination of the past [...] It also means an intensive exchange with living present-day Judaism."[15]

Modern concept for the Old Synagogue

The former synagogue should be a place where visitors, mostly non-Jews, can see, learn and experience the diversity of Judaism, laugh humorously together with Jews (unfortunately only virtually) about Jews and get to know the idiosyncrasies of the very different types of Jewishness. In other words: not only talk about "dead Jews" who once lived in Germany but focus more on today's Jewish citizens. The new concept was also about breaking down clichés, prejudices and rigid images of "the" Jew or at least to irritate. A good example is the "orthodox Jew" whose appearance at times seems to outshine the perception of Jewish diversity. It still wasn't until 2003 that a large group of people came together for the first time who had understood and internalised the basic idea of the concept.

It wasn't a coincidence, however, that during the discussion concerning the programme to re-focus the Old Synagogue as a house of Jewish culture, local historians once again warned of an alleged "dehistoricization" of the house. It looked as if the historians were afraid of losing their dominant position with regard to interpreting and shaping the institution in the case of a programmatic reorientation of the Old Synagogue. Against this backdrop arose the honest need to visibly and discernibly separate the Old Synagogue from the numerous other Memorials for Nazi Victims and take it into a new and different direction by founding a House of Jewish Culture. Since then, the house's work has not only focussed on coming to terms with the Nazi past (and giving Germans a "guilty conscience") but on the history, diversity, self-irony and tradition of the subjects who built this house, in short: who made it their liturgical and social centre. It was equally important to show and display a living and vibrant Judaism not only to people in Germany but also to the large number of Jewish immigrants from Community of Independent (former communist) States countries.[16]

The booklet to the new permanent exhibition published in July 2010 as well as my ideas that led to the programmatic reorientation of the Old Synagogue are, of course, also engulfed in the constant flow of history. I can therefore only give a brief outlook of things to come..

Outlook

In the face of a new German reality after September 2015, when a large number of immigrants from Muslim countries were invited to come to Germany, my look back to the past discourses on "commemoration" or "remembrance" may seem a bit anachronistic. It may well be that the Old Synagogue's entire existence is called into question in the future as, in an ever more heterogeneous society, the consensual process of creating an identity will be fundamentally called into question or even made impossible. To make matters worse for a *House of Jewish Culture,* many immigrants and the culture they bring with them have been strongly shaped by an enmity towards Jews and religious antisemitism. It is difficult to fully assess at present what the consequences of this development will be for the Old Synagogue over the next few years.

We can already see, however, that engagement with Germany's Jewish history which up until now has been at the centre of the remembrance discourse – which has, in large parts, helped to shape German identity – has noticeably been losing ground to a shifting (political) focus on the growing Muslim population in Germany. Therefore, the threat is not to be dismissed out of hand that the *House of Jewish Culture* could become a House of World Cultures. This, however, would not only mean the repeated destruction of the cultural heritage embodied by the location that is the Old Synagogue. It would also mean giving up a part of Germany's rich cultural heritage itself. As someone who actively lives her Jewish identity, such a scenario makes me fear mostly for Germany itself.

Footnotes

1. See also König, Helmut: "Vom Beschweigen zum Erinnern. Shoah und Zweiter Weltkrieg im politischen Bewußtsein der Bundesrepublik", in: Osteuropa, issue 4-6/2005
2. Koselleck, Reinhart: "Nachdenken über Geschichtsschreibung, Dankrede zur Verleihung des Sigmund-Freud-Preises", in: Neue Zürcher Zeitung, 22 November 1999
3. See detailed article by Jureit, Ulrike: "Vom Zwang zu erinnern", in: "Merkur. Deutsche Zeitschrift für europäisches Denken", issue 2-61. February 2007, p. 158–163
4. Ibid.
5. See Arendt, Hannah: "Besuch in Deutschland", 1950 English version, 1986, 2/1993 German version.
6. VVN-BdA e.V. is the "Vereinigung der Verfolgten des Naziregimes – Bund der Antifaschistinnen und Antifaschisten" with its headquarters in Berlin
7. Note the, for this time, typical order: as if the resistance came first, and only then the persecution
8. The modern term would be "integrate"
9. Siebeck, Cornelia: "Verräumlichtes Gedächtnis. Gedenkstätten an historischen Orten: „Topolatrie" oder „Orte von Belang"?" Uploaded as a PDF file in 2013 https://www.academia.edu/9751253/_2013_Verräumlichtes_Gedächtnis._Gedenkstätten_an_historischen_Orten_Topolatrie_oder_Orte_von_Belang_
10. Korff, Gottfried: "Museumsdinge, deponieren – exponieren", ed.s Martina Eberspächer, Gudrun Marlene König and Bernhard Tschofen, Vienna 2/2007
11. Psychologie Heute 3/27, March 2000, p. 3
12. Aleida, Assmann: "Der lange Schatten der Vergangenheit. Erinnerungskultur und Erinnerungspolitik", Munich 2006, p. 231
13. Yerushalmi, Yosef Hayim: Zakhor. Jewish history and Jewish memory, New York, ²1986, p. 105–117
14. Yerushalmi, Yosef Hayim: Zakhor. Jewish history and Jewish memory, New York, ²1986
15. Boschki, Reinhold/Gerhards, Albert (Ed.): "Erinnerungskultur in der pluralen Gesellschaft – Neue Perspektiven für den christlich-jüdischen Dialog", Paderborn, 2010
16. König, Helmut: "Paradoxien der Erinnerung", in: Osteuropa, issue 4/2011: "Amnesie international. Justitia, Memoria, Judaika", p. 43–54

"... Germany's most illustrious synagogue building!"

The Architecture of the Old Synagogue in Essen. Observations on the historic building

Dorothee Rauhut

No matter whether we look at historic sources or refer back to architectural observations, people have always been full of praise for the Old Synagogue building. Indeed it has been extolled as "magnificent, remarkable, excellent" and even as "renowned".[1] Such evaluations are the result of a number of specific features.

The Old Synagogue in Essen was designed by Professor Edmund Körner and officially opened on the 25th September 1913. At the time it was built it was one of the largest freestanding synagogues in Germany. It could hold around 1,500 people. In addition its imposing copper dome (it had a diameter of ca 30 metres), was one of the largest to have ever been placed on a synagogue. Even today it can still be seen from afar. The highly balanced, clearly structured design was utterly unique. As such it was a patent demonstration that modern synagogue designs could be a success. Furthermore placing the main room on an almost circular layout seemed an almost daring idea, for up till then this shape was an exception. It was not only the design of the synagogue that earned so much praise but also its rich and splendidly decorated furnishings. Whereas relief stones, inscriptions and decorative bands are still visible on the exterior of the building, a huge amount of decorations in the interior have now been lost for ever, with the exception of a few reconstructions.

At the time it was built the synagogue in Essen aroused great attention. One of the scholarly assessments reads as follows: "The Essen synagogue marked the climax of a development that took only a few years from the start of the century, and which tried to find its own architectural style without directly referring to designs used in mediaeval synagogues or the Arab Orient" [2]

The question arises as to how the architect designed the building in order to achieve such a result. What examples of former synagogues was Körner using for his ideas? What were the wishes and demands formulated by the Jewish community in Essen at the time? And what impulses did they give him? Körner's synagogue was so successful that he received further commissions from the city: these must also be taken into account if we are to get a more comprehensive idea of the architect's work.

Planning the new building

Even today the monumental size of the synagogue can give us some idea of the large, influential community that must have been responsible for its construction. In 1913 the Jewish community in Essen – it had increased alongside the general growth in the population caused by industrialisation – comprised around 3,700 members. The previous synagogue at II. Weberstraße (today Gerswidastraße) had opened in 1871, but by 1894 it had simply become too small. This was the year in which Rabbi Salomon Samuel had taken up his office in Essen. Two years later, in 1896, the population reached 100,000, thereby giving it the status of a major city. The Lord Mayor at the time, a man by the name of Erich Zweigert, remarked dryly that this did not necessarily make Essen a major city, but it was indeed a large city. True a large number of people lived in the city. Nonetheless it did not give the impression of a major city because it lacked a suitable infrastructure and administration, not to speak of cultural institutions. We only have to take ourselves back to this time in order to be able to appreciate the efforts of local politicians to persuade businesses and organisations to set down roots in the city. For example, major companies like the RWE AG, the Rheinland-Westphalian Coal Syndicate, the Ruhr Valley Locks Association and the Goldschmidt Brothers Company all decided to have their headquarters in Essen. The upshot was the construction of representative buildings to upgrade the image of the city. To name just a few examples: the town hall was rebuilt in 1887, the central station rebuilt in 1902, and the Concert Hall (Saalbau) in 1904. The Grillo theatre opened in 1892, the Church of the Cross in 1896 and the Church of the Redeemer in 1909, both of which were monumental church buildings. Theodor Althoff's department store opened in 1912, the Trading Centre (Handelshof) in 1913, and the new law court in Zweigertstraße, one of the largest court buildings in Prussia, officially opened in May 1913. Thus when the synagogue opened in September that year it put the finishing touch, so to speak, on a range of remarkable buildings completed before the First World War.

    I should first like to throw some light on the developments which led to the planning of the synagogue. The prosperity of the city had given rise to improved educational and commercial conditions for its Jewish citizens. A few Jewish families became wealthy, many Jews were active in cultural life and the numerous Jewish societies; indeed some of them were even members of the City Council. In 1902, when it was clear that their synagogue had become too small, the community bought up an old restaurant in Kastanienallee called "Die Rothenburg", as a temporary addition to accommodate the congregation. At the same time it kept an eye out for a new plot of land close to the old city centre, where 80% of Jews lived. The search ended in 1903 when Lord Mayor Zweigert offered the community a plot of land at the old Steeler Tor. In many respects the site was highly suitable for a new synagogue. It covered around 3000 m², which made it large enough; and it was situated on a slope tapering down from Steeler Straße to Alfredistraße, the former being one of the main roads leading to the city centre. Truly a prominent position. Similar sites were usual in ancient times. Whenever the situation allowed: a synagogue would preferably be situated at the highest point in a town, beside a river or a spring. When transposed to a 20th century city, this was indeed a comparably worthy location. And by contrast with a synagogue that was simply part of a row of houses, the Jewish community now had the opportunity to construct a freestanding, representative building.

Negotiations to purchase the plot of land were completed in 1904, and on 1st April 1905 the community purchased the building site for 180,000 Marks. In 1907 the design was put out for competitive tender throughout the whole of Germany. As a result 72 designs were submitted. The jury consisted of honourable personalities from the city administration and the Jewish community, including the chair of the community, Isaak Hirschland, Lord Mayor Holle, the architects Georg Frentzen and Johannes Otzen, who had been Körner's teacher since 1906. These were joined by the Aldermen Guckuck and Robert Schmohl, both of whom were highly regarded architects. The selection of a jury consisting of such prominent personalities demonstrated the importance the city attached to the building. As a result, on 12th June 1908 Edmund Körner was commissioned to design the new synagogue and took up the post of head of the City Construction Design Department.

In order to truly appreciate the significance of the commission it is necessary to take account of its scale. It was intended not simply as a synagogue but a community centre, the main building of which should have an additional entrance hall, a forecourt, a weekday synagogue with a separate entrance, a garden and a house for the rabbi.

Körner was not the sole victor in the tendering competition. The jury had not been able to agree on the final decision and, as a result, it decided to award three first prizes. The other two went to the Boswau & Knauer architecture office and the Berlin architect, Johannes Otto.

It is an interesting fact that Körner was only entrusted with building the synagogue on condition that he reworked his design; and it is precisely these changes that reveal the intentions behind the building.

Körner's initial design for the synagogue in 1909 (see the archive for the illustration) shows a rather squat building with a tapering dome, the bottom edge of which is intersected by three triangular dormers. Beneath this are six large circular windows each of which contain a Star of David. The forecourt was a relatively flat enclosure. The desired reworking was clearly intended to make it more monumental. The building was enlarged and made higher. A comparison reveals that the design entered by Boswau & Knauer (for the illustration see the archive in the Old Synagogue Essen) was more monumental from the very start, and one may speculate why the jury did not decide in its favour. Indeed one might even suspect that Johannes Otzen in particular had argued in favour of his former student. The critical factors supporting this view were the huge amount of space and the circular layout of the main room as outlined by Boswau & Knauer, when compared to Körner's design. Both features were retained.

What did the monumentalisation look like precisely? In Körner's initial design the main room is topped by a mighty rectangular tower with a dome, so to say, on a plinth. It was compared to the Monument to the Battle of the Nations in Leipzig, which was incidentally also completed in 1913. The synagogue's closeness to monument buildings – a few Bismarck towers could also be invoked – demonstrates that the jury who selected the winning design were keen on it being noticed and remembered, as well as giving an impression of permanence.

The dome was made even higher by giving it a tambour interspersed with arched windows. This is where the dome, which was basically made up of two cupola shells, was finally positioned. The inner shell was around 26 metres high – its diameter was around 30 metres – and the outer shell around 34 metres high. Körner also changed the shape of the dome. Previously it was to have been round with a smooth surface and a Star of David at the tip. But now the surface was given a new structure of ridges and its lower area swung out in a concave fashion. We are familiar with such a dome shape from, say, Baroque city castles. Hence, despite all the conspicuously new features in the building, the final decision went in favour of a tried-and-trusted architectural motif.

The design of the windows was based on a similar philosophy. Körner replaced the round windows containing the portrait of the Star of David by arched windows. These accentuated the vertical dimensions of the building and were reminiscent of Romanic designs. The Stars of David, each of which would have filled the whole window, were abandoned completely.

The thrust forces of the mighty dome demanded stair towers that now gave the synagogue a monumental, formidable character. This monumental style (similar to fortresses, for example), is further accentuated by the surrounding plinth and the sparsely punctuated, structured masonry made of roughly hewn rock. Hence the wording in the deed for the laying of the foundation stone on 11th July 1911; "may [the synagogue] tower into distant times; ...".[3]

This impression, evoked by a cladding of roughly hewn ashlar masonry somewhat belies the fact that the synagogue stands on a reinforced concrete structure, just like a modern building. Only when the 1909 design was reworked, was it decided to use rustic concha-limestone for the walls in order to break up the smoothly worked surface intermittently.

Finally Körner added flattened round side annexes to the central block to give more weight to the forecourt. By contrast to the first outline he surrounded it with a higher wall that opened inwards into an arcade passage. This forecourt is a harmonious counterweight to the mighty synagogue and gives a balance to the staggering of the building, for which Körner was highly praised on many occasions.

The exterior of the building

If we look at old photographs showing the synagogue and its forecourt we might be tempted to compare the building with a sphinx (ill. see Klapheck), lying between the two streets that meet at an acute angle, with its arms (in this case the two outer walls and the surroundings of the forecourt) appearing to reach out towards the city centre. Seen from the front the individual buildings seem to be stacked up, indeed almost piled up like a tower behind one another. Here the dome roofs are an important linking element.

Entrance pavilions flanking the door to the forecourt were covered by dome-like hoods. The roofed side corridors in the forecourt led to the synagogue entrance in a gentle convex arch. Here the roof over the porch is relatively flat although it rises to a peak on both sides – again another dome motif! The entrance hall with its large tympanum rises up behind the porch, and is rounded off by a saddle roof. Each of the side towers rise up at the same height: originally they also had cupola roofs. The apex of the building is the large dome on the main room at its centre.

Thus the building seems to swing upwards step-by-step, as it were, and this impression is strengthened by the domed roof areas. The impression that Körner had initially made a model of the building is particularly accurate, because the architect did not work exclusively at his drawing board with a pencil and a ruler but modelled with his hands. "Körner did indeed work with clay models in his atelier."[4] One of these models was of the synagogue in Essen.

If we now look more closely at the surface of the synagogue walls, we can see that they are structured in a very special manner. Plaster strips alternate with cornices, roughly hewn ashlar frames with smooth surfaces, and the façade is decorated with relief stones in prominent positions. The stones show grapes and vine leaves, pine cones, pomegranates, ears of wheat, and lions – all of them symbols related to Jewish culture. Grapes symbolise the fertility of Israel; pine cones, ears of wheat and pomegranates with their many seeds symbolise the richness of life. These motifs also decorated ancient synagogue buildings in Palestine, a land that was subject to intensive archaeological diggings from the end of the 19th century. From the 1880s onwards the results became more and more known in Europe and societies met up to discuss Jewish art and culture: their new discoveries also reached an interested general public. In 1887 an exhibition of Anglo-Jewish cultural assets took place in the Royal Albert Hall in London, and these were documented in a catalogue. In 1897 a "Museum for the Conservation of Jewish Antiquities" opened in Vienna, and in the same year Heinrich Frauberger, the director of the Museum of Applied Art in Düsseldorf, founded the "Society for Research into Jewish Arts Monuments" that had its headquarters in Frankfurt. In 1908 the society presented an exhibition in Düsseldorf.

For his part Körner maintained contacts with Berlin and "(...) by 1909 at the latest, segments of friezes and ornamented stones were exhibited in the Royal Museums in Berlin"[5]

These developments made up a wealth of information on which Körner could draw. He was able to fall back on tangible models of Jewish tradition, although he clearly stayed close to a building handbook written by Cornelius Gurlitt in 1906, which recommended decorating modern synagogues with portraits of vine leaves, grapes and ears of wheat.

Körner gave particular attention to the design of the tympanum. The roof was crowned with the tablets containing the Ten Commandments, a common symbol of the Jewish religion, which from the end of the 19th century frequently identified buildings as synagogues, just as crosses were used to identify Christian churches. Directly beneath, there is a medallion showing hands held in benediction. The reliefs are made even more prominent by the background of smoothly polished concha-limestone. Under this, in a rectangular area we can see a large round window containing a portrait of a Menorah. This seven branched candelabra was the eternal light in the Jerusalem Temple and is the oldest and most important symbol of Judaism. For this reason it was portrayed directly above the entrance portal. Comparable arrangements can be found in ancient synagogues like, for example, the synagogue in Nawa that was built in the 4th century. At the same time the large round window in Essen is reminiscent of rose windows in the west wings of Gothic cathedrals.

The window is flanked by inscriptions in Hebrew and German that are also addressed to non-Jewish persons. They read: "And thou shalt love thy neighbour as thyself, I am the Lord" (a mitzvah or commandment from the Old Testament) and: "Verily my house shall be called a house of prayer for all peoples." This wish was fulfilled at the official opening of the synagogue when Salomon Samuel made the following remark: "The finest opening this house could receive is provided by the joyful participation of so many distinguished, high-ranking guests of all confessions, (...)."[6]

The entrance to the synagogue

The long triangular plot of ground on which the synagogue is built has often been compared with the shape of a piece of cake. Despite the difficulty, this shape had a particular attraction in that it lay in a West-East direction. Thus the entrance to the synagogue in the West lies at the narrowest and deepest point of the site, from where it rises up to the Torah ark at the East wall of the main room. Here a person at prayer would be facing east towards Jerusalem. In doing so, Körner designed the rooms on the east side in such a way as to trigger off a powerful impression of greater breadth and width. Thus the site is based on a clear axis and spatial augmentation, and it is well worth following this path attentively.

Visitors originally arrived at the forecourt of the synagogue where they were faced with the first steps upwards into the building. Inscriptions were written on the flattened surface of the columns at the doorway to the forecourt to welcome and address the approaching guests.

True, the synagogue only suffered relatively little harm from air raids during the Second World War that only damaged the forecourt and the domed roofs over the staircase towers. Nonetheless the city of Essen decided to dispose of the demolished forecourt after the war in order to make room for a large road round the inner-city area. The domed roofs were replaced by relatively flat roofs.

Only a few city synagogues contained a forecourt in the 19th and early 20th century, since there was frequently insufficient room in densely populated inner-city areas. In Essen the forecourt covered an area of around 400 m. One reason for this was to allow the Jewish community to present itself prominently by means of such a synagogue complex.

The forecourt of the Essen synagogue widened out to the gateway and its walls curved slightly outwards. By contrast the west facade of the synagogue has a concave curve pointing towards the interior of the building. (This is an extremely uncommon architectural motif, although it can be compared to the entrance facade of the Mannheim Art Hall designed by Hermann Billing in 1907). The large flight of steps exactly mirrors the dynamics of the curve. In this manner the steps guide visitors into the building, especially when we consider that the columns at the entrance to the forecourt were opposite those at the synagogue gateway.

But the forecourt had a further important function. This was where visitors entered the synagogue for the first time and had the opportunity of throwing off their everyday cares, so to speak, and meeting other members of the community. The forecourt was thus a place to stop and rest a while. Körner underlined this aim literally by designing arcade arches whose pillars were arranged with corner-stones placed parallel to one another. This resulted in consciously arranged cross-connecting lines to counterbalance the suggested longitudinal direction. This design highlights an ambivalence that often recurs in the whole building in various forms, and which gives the synagogue its particular fascination.

The design of the gateway with its deep embrasure and many relief tapes is highly significant. It is very reminiscent of tympana in Roman churches, the difference here being that the motifs refer to Jewish religion and culture. Columns with the heads of lions and pillars subdivide the entrance area with three heavy double-wing bronze doors. Each door was decorated with six circular medallions that were originally precious reliefs with enamellings and semi-precious stones. The outer doors carry the symbols of the twelve tribes and the central doors show motifs of Jewish symbols like the Crown of Erudition and hands in benediction. They are there to remind Jewish visitors of their origins and identity before they enter the synagogue. There again the door handles are shaped in the form of stylised ram's horns – shofar horns – that play an important role in the Jewish holidays, Rosh ha-Shanah and Yom Kippur.

The path proceeds further through the doorway into a narrow porch. It was relatively low and only dimly lit by comparatively small windows. The metal rods in the windows can be understood as a reference to the Jerusalem Temple, where the Bible reads: "And for the house he made windows with recessed bevelled frames." (I. Kings. 6,4)

Steps now lead to the doors of the entrance hall. In classical times this was known as the "vestibulum" and in Byzantine times as the "narthex". It was a place of greeting and preparation for services and other ceremonies, as well as containing a men's wardrobe. In Essen it is placed crosswise to the main room and subdivided into three spatial segments by powerful pillars. Here the ambivalence in the composition is similar to that in the forecourt. Alone the clear emphasis on the lateral axis invites visitors to pause and reflect for a moment. Furthermore the roof is relatively low and the room dimly lit. Hence anyone entering the area is willy-nilly forced to slow down a little. On the other hand the way forward is now clearly indicated because the three doors in the entrance hall are parallel to those leading into the main room.

To differentiate between the rather more practical functions of the entrance hall and the central significance of the main room, and at the same time to emphasise even more strongly the splendour of the main room, Körner furnished the entrance hall sparingly and only gave it a few decorations. Three quatrefoil windows were arranged over each of the doors and the coffered ceiling was dominated by plain geometrical circles and squares. Originally the pillars had sconces and wall wells. The latter were there for ritual hand washing – an association with the molten sea in the Jerusalem Temple.

Körner adopted the style of the entrance hall once more in his design for the weekday synagogue on the basement floor. It too had a similar coffered ceiling and was decorated in a somewhat restrained fashion with glass paintings and tiny mosaics. In addition there was a Torah ark that could be seen as an abbreviation of that in the main room. The equivalence in the design of the rooms supported the shared identity of the individual spaces in the building. (For an illustration of the entrance hall and weekday synagogue, see Klapheck).

The main room

The word "synagogue" comes from the Greek and means "place of meeting" (Bet ha-Knesset). As such the synagogue is the centre of the community where people meet for services, a place of learning (Bet ha-Midrash) and a place of prayer (Bet ha-Tefila). Before Jewish emancipation synagogues were used as lodging places and law courts. The variety of functions prevented the development of an ideal form and a typical architectural shape. In the final analysis every space with an undamaged Torah scroll kept in a Torah ark (Aron ha-Kodesch) could be used as a synagogue. In ancient times people preferred to keep the Torah ark near a wall pointing towards Jerusalem, and a raised lectern known as a bimah was necessary for readings from the Torah. In order to ensure that everybody in the congregation could hear what was being read out it seemed logical to place the bimah in the centre of the room. On the one hand the shape of the synagogue was best realised by a longitudinal house in the direction of Jerusalem: on the other hand the best place for the bimah was considered to be in the centre of the room. Initially the one seemed to contradict the other.

But Körner exploited both potentialities. Hence we are able to observe a further moment of tension in the Essen synagogue; the ambivalence between the direction of the synagogue and the central space within the building. The idea behind the central building is all the more interesting because a bimah was never placed in the centre of the main room in Essen. True, Körner's basic design for the central room was circular but he opened up the circle on two sides by adding barrel vaults in the west and east. The vault in the west formed the entrance to the main room; the vault in the east was placed above the Torah ark and was consciously deeper than that in the west. The resulting impression of depth gives the building a direction leading rigorously to the Torah ark. Since this should be the main focus of attention it is underlined by its impressive size and a stairway that raises it above the ground level in the main room. The first steps lead to a podium on which stands the lectern that is equally used by the prayer leader, and as a bimah for the person reading from the Torah.

Following the start of the Jewish reform movement the bimah began to be located at the east wall directly next to the Torah ark. Hence this particular location is also a sign of a reform synagogue. "Thus the thousand-year old conflicts about synagogue spaces were set aside in this synagogue." [7] For the synagogue in Essen the relocation of the bimah from the east wall to the centre of the room was a basic precondition for the building's axial alignment. Körner extended this axis to the Torah ark right down to the last detail. People entering the main room from the vestibule first find themselves standing beneath the former women's gallery. Initially this blocks the view and prevents us from looking up at the dome. Instead the relatively low gallery takes up the circular shape of the main room and describes a U-shaped arch. The gaze of the viewer follows this horizontal line and is led to the monumental Torah ark that rises up at the centre of the east wall, and whose height is further accentuated by its vertical lines. Thus, on entering the room our gaze is first drawn towards the Torah ark.

Körner repeated the architectural lines very beautifully in his decorations in the gallery. A zigzag frieze runs along the balustrade, simultaneously leading our gaze rhythmically downwards. Even beneath the gallery there were three further friezes, all of them staggered, which took up the circular dynamics (for the illustration, see Klapheck).

If we now step out from beneath the gallery, the size and height of the main room and its dome seem even more impressive. The modern construction of the cupola as a self-sustaining concrete shell made it unnecessary to have supporting columns. The view of the cupola remained clear although a large wheel chandelier once hung in the centre of the room, along with many other individual lamps. In many respects the main room is the architectural climax of the whole building, not only because it is the largest and highest room and is crowned by the huge dome, but also because of the light from the large arched windows over the gallery which illuminates the space and its splendid, precious furnishings.

In choosing a circle for the basic design of the main room, Körner selected an ideal geometric shape. From time immemorial a circle has been regarded as a harmonious basic shape; and in sacred areas as a divine symbol of perfection. The congregation in the synagogue in Essen is surrounded – one might even say, protected – by rounded walls. The importance of the circular shape is hinted at by its repetition in the wheel chandelier, the surrounding windows and finally in the large round dome ornamented with mosaics arranged in concentric circles, with the Star of David at its peak.

Despite the strong emphasis on circular shapes the members of the Jewish community in Essen did not gather in a large circle. The original arrangement of benches in straight rows gives this the lie. People came here to congregate before the Torah ark and this was intended to be the centre of their attention.

It is noticeable that the basic structure of the Torah ark resembles the facade of a temple. Two large columns bear an architrave (for the illustration, see Klapheck). The doors of the ark are flanked by two columns, as if an ark has been placed within the temple itself, although this is merely a sign of the Ark of the Covenant. Ancient coins, reliefs and frescos in old synagogues did indeed often portray the Torah ark in association with the entrance to the temple. In Essen the Torah ark and the image of the temple are virtually one. This connection is plausible in so far as the Jerusalem Temple was once regarded as the House of God. By contrast the Torah in the synagogue evokes the word of God and, as such represents the presence of God. The inscription in the mosaic on the Torah ark seems to confirm this ("Know before whom thou standest"), and reflects the opinion of Salomon Samuel who regarded the synagogue as a "House of God" when he wrote:

"Here a house of God has been completed, which in every respect exceeds and outshines all its predecessors; it demands that we pause for a moment and envisage everything that is included in such a splendid framework, envisage everything that should be contained in such a precious vessel." [8]

The lions on the shrine also fit this concept, for they can also be found on many ancient Torah arks. For one, the lion is the symbol of the Tribe of Judah. On the other hand it is known in an apotropaic function as a guard in ancient cultures. If we take a closer look at the stance of the three lions on the Torah ark in the Old Synagogue, which look alertly in three directions it is clear that they are symbolically guarding the Torah, and simultaneously symbolise the power of the Torah as interpreted by Jewish tradition. The depictions of plant tendrils also refer back to the Torah, for traditional Jewish ideas equate the Torah (rods) with the Tree of Life. Hence vegetable motifs frequently occur in the context of the Torah as symbols of life-giving powers.

The shell-shaped canopy over the doors to the ark also has parallels in ancient portraits for antique images reveal that a shell was the symbol of all things related to the Torah. Finally the bronze sliding doors are decorated with medallions, each of which show the crown of the Torah, of which it is said that anyone who studies the Torah hard enough can possess it. Here every single person is addressed and referred to the importance of the Torah as a "directive" in everyday life.

A further more basic and extremely attractive aspect is the fact that Körner not only linked his work to ancient Jewish art but also to the work of a contemporary Jewish artist, Ephraim Moses Lilien (1874–1925). For one, a Torah curtain originally hung in front of the ark. It carried the inscription "To honour and extol the Torah" and was embroidered with portraits of lions and medallions, containing mostly stars and the Menorah. Comparisons show that Körner took these motifs from drawings by Lilien who was a well known, popular Jugendstil artist at the time. Secondly, Körner drew on Lilien's work when he designed the bronze doors at the synagogue entrance. In 1907 Lilien had been commissioned by the Georg Westermann publishing house in Braunschweig to illustrate a ten-volume edition of the Bible. In it he surrounded one of the pages with the emblems of the Twelve Tribes of Israel. Körner transposed these emblems into the circular shape of the medallions, for the most part using Lilien's designs.

What was the aim of giving priority to a modern Jewish artist, by quoting his motifs on the entrance doors? Lilien's illustrations had set new standards for Jewish art in his time. He had worked for the magazine "Die Jugend" in Munich and at the Bezalel Academy of Applied Arts in Jerusalem. Hence he was relatively famous and enjoyed recognition in the outside world. In this way transferring his designs into the furnishings of the synagogue was a way to guarantee the quality, topicality and modernity of the building. It also expressed the wishes of the people who commissioned the building – the Rabbi and the Jewish community in Essen – that it was important to refer back to Jewish tradition, and equally important to maintain and value the progress of Jewish art since then. Could there have been a better way than this of mediating the long duration of Jewish history and the achievements of contemporary Jewish art in a single image? The Rabbi wanted a freestanding Jewish building and was clearly satisfied with the result: a successful blend of tradition and modernity.

An idea of the original furnishings

It is difficult for today's visitors to fully appreciate the original splendour in the interior of the synagogue. A huge number of mosaic medallions with unique iconographic designs decorated the main room. Today their original position is indicated by nothing more than white circles. Alone in the Eastern vault six rows of 18 medallions were used to decorate the Torah ark. Behind the Torah ark on the East wall there were seven emblems arranged in the form of an arch; in the gussets beneath the dome two linked medallions contained inscriptions with texts from the Psalms. Further mosaic medallions could be seen above the large arched window, in the deep window soffits and the west vault: whereas smaller mosaic portraits decorated the balustrade of the women's gallery and its pillars.

Today it is also impossible to reconstruct the colourful impression of the interior. Sources on the way in which the plaster was coloured – a coloured gouache drawing and descriptions in the press at the time the synagogue was opened – are subjective. Körner himself described his ideas in letters to the Puhl & Wagner firm in Berlin, which had been entrusted with the mosaics. Here he said that the plaster in the interior should be given a greyish-green shade, the basic colour of the ornaments should be somewhat darker and the window niches should be painted in a strong dull green (for an illustration, see Klapheck).

Light played a decisive role in the overall impression of the synagogue interior. Originally it fell through colourfully designed windows. The six main Jewish holidays were portrayed in the large arched windows above the gallery, and in the smaller windows beneath the gallery there were scenes from the Torah. The result was a play of colourful light reflected by the mosaic stones, whereby individual design elements reflected and heightened the overall effect. Thus the composition of the colours was the result of a contrast between the cooler colour on the plaster and the somewhat warmer colours in the mosaics and images in the windows.

Two seven branched candelabras on either side of the Torah ark, and the Eternal Light hanging in front of the shrine, were important reminders of the Jerusalem Temple. Whereas Körner aligned the seven-branched candelabra in a stringently vertical direction to the design of the Torah ark and decorated it with medallions and Jewish symbols, the Eternal Light was the work of a Jugendstil artist by the name of Theodor Wende.

The sound of the organ filled the main room during services and festive occasions: a huge organ was placed above the Torah ark – in 1913 it was even the largest organ in Essen – and there was enough room for the community choir to gather on the organ gallery.

Whereas we can only get a vague overall idea of the interior, a monograph by Richard Klapheck (1914) has enabled us to inherit drawings of the motifs in the large emblems. For example, the mosaics contained portraits of temple reconstructions, the Menorah, the brazen sea and the cauldron cart, the tablets with the Ten Commandments, interwoven candles, crowns, palms and grapes, as well as a variety of animal symbols and rosettes.

All these symbols developed in ancient times when they were initially and frequently used on coins. One of the first was the Menorah, but vines and vine leaves were already to be seen in the years before the birth of Christ. In the first few decades CE we can find symbolic examples of ears of wheat, pomegranates, palm branches, etrogs and chalices. The facade of the Temple was also an important motif after the Bar Kokhba revolt (132–135 CE). The repertoire of religious symbols soon spread throughout the whole of the Jewish diaspora. It kept alive the memory of the past and formed the basis of Jewish art.

Several examples in the synagogue in Essen show that Körner fell back on ancient examples in his designs for the mosaic medallions. Alongside the reliefs and coins which served as the sources, there were also gold glasses and glass bottoms. Such glasses were made by Jews between the third and the fifth century CE. They were highly artistic. Their special value lay in the fact that the bottom of the glass was lined with gold leaf or pigments and then sealed with a further layer of transparent glass. The precious glasses, and sometimes only the glass bottoms, were used as everyday items in rites, and also as burial objects as wall decorations. There is a huge range of motifs, frequently of objects used in temples and rites. As for the use of these motifs in the Essen synagogue, it seems remarkable that although they had become public knowledge from archaeological finds in the second half of the 19th century this was the first time they had been used in the furnishings of a synagogue. Indeed the findings only aroused interest around the start of the 20th century, when Jewish art began to become a more topical subject of discussion. It was precisely this interest that was behind the selection of images made by the Jewish community and above all, their Rabbi, Salomon Samuel. We can find a reference to them in the following passage from Samuel's writings: "In the 90s German Jews began to take a more active part in public life. (…), our self-confidence returned, and (…) our congregations were inspired by the indestructible will to create a new Jewish renaissance".[9]

True, the architect was responsible for designing the furnishings in the interior, but Rabbi Samuel was the decisive factor in deciding on the ideas and contents. There again, his knowledge surely came from his acquaintance with Heinrich Frauberger, the director of the Düsseldorf Museum of Applied Arts. It was also enriched by the "Society for Research into Jewish Artistic Monuments" which gave the Rabbi the opportunity to acquaint himself with the latest findings. Last not least he collaborated on an exhibition that also displayed gold glass bottoms.

Körner's initial designs for the interior were created as early as 1910, when the motifs, patterns and forms in the area around the Torah ark and the windows, the doors and also in the decorations, were different from those that were later realised. At the time he still had to think out a detailed plan! The discussions between the architect and the Rabbi seem to have been conducted in a harmonious and fruitful way, for Körner – he was not Jewish himself but had been baptised as a Catholic – wrote the following about it: "in my conscious desire to avoid an arbitrary new ornamentation and to revive memories of the ornamental decorations in the rich legacy of Jewish culture I was continually provided with objective guidance and goodwill by Dr. Samuel and Dr. Cohn, in an area of which I had very little knowledge to date. I should like to express my special gratitude to Herr Dr. Samuel for referring me to the relevant literature and other sources – in so far as they were available – and equally for his advice in the selection of the motifs that I had thought out for each particular aim."[10]

Körner "revived memories" by transferring the original motifs into his work in a simplified form but with a greater exactitude, thereby giving them a modern style. The Berlin company Puhl & Wagner were also responsible for making the emblems in the mosaic plaster and the contrast between the dull coloured plaster background and the mosaic stones served to heighten the brilliance of the mosaic portraits. It is easy to imagine that they gave an exceptional splendour to the interior which must have made a surprising and festive contrast to the compact exterior of the synagogue.

Let us now turn to the windows. The portraits of the Jewish holidays in the large arched windows above the women's gallery corresponded wonderfully with the contents of the circular main room. Following the direction in which Hebrew is read, the holidays portrayed in the six windows were arranged from right to left, beginning with the image of Shabbat and continuing in chronological order throughout the year. Accordingly the circle in the floor plan followed the annual cycle!

The portrait of Shabbat as the highest Jewish holiday was allocated to the first window on the south-west side. This was followed by the Pessach (Passover) and Shavuot (Revelation of the Torah), and on the north-west side by Rosh ha-Shanah, Yom Kippur and finally Sukkoth, the Feast of Tabernacles. The annual reading from the Torah ends with the final festivity in autumn when it immediately begins anew from the start.

In 1913 the idea of portraying Jewish holidays in synagogue windows was not at all new. Ten years previously the Rabbi Immanuel Löw had chosen this theme for the windows in the large synagogue in the town of Szeged in Hungary. But when we compare them to Körner's designs in Essen the latter are more simplified and modern in style and in their choice of colours. The windows for the synagogue in Essen were made by the Berlin glass painter Gottfried Heinersdorff. In a letter written to him on 8th January 1913 Körner mentioned a "possible restriction in the amount of colours" and wanted him "to only emphasise the individual motifs in colour". [11] Nevertheless the theme was dealt with in a much more comprehensive manner in Essen than in Szeged, when the large arched windows were arranged in individual zones. The four tall slender windows in the central middle zone show symbols, liturgical and cult objects related to the corresponding holiday, including an appropriate quotation from the Torah (at Rosh ha-Shanah from one of the Psalms), along with motifs like the Menorah, chalices, stars, hands in benediction and the tablets with the Ten Commandments that decorated the lower segments of the windows and the circular segments in the round arches above.

We must regard the original agenda to decorate the synagogue in Essen with reliefs, mosaics and images in the windows as a single unit corresponding to a "Gesamtkunstwerk" because of the variety of references in their content and artistic composition. That they would be regarded as particularly beautiful was not only a matter of prestige. The aesthetics went hand-in-hand with the intention of making a visit to the synagogue an attractive experience. For, whilst the preceding synagogue was in use, the Rabbi noticed that some members of the synagogue community had been alienated by the building, and he regretted that weddings were scarcely celebrated there any more. Furthermore the themes from Jewish history, their rites and customs were based on didactic considerations. They were intended to mediate Jewish identity and self-confidence for, as Samuel wrote: "to be quite honest the best way to strengthen Jewish self-confidence is through knowledge of Judaism."[12]

Some aspects of the development of synagogue buildings

What should a synagogue look like at the start of the 20th century? What examples and what ideas were there? In an essay written in 1908 the Essen Rabbi, Salomon Samuel remarked critically that many synagogues in German cities increasingly had Romanic or Gothic shapes, and could only be distinguished from churches by "appearing to have planted a Star of David on the top". He disliked this just as much as the "onion-like" cupolas on the Essen synagogue completed in 1871 to which he preferred an "oriental style". He summed up by saying that a cult building should be a "character building" and a synagogue has the right to claim to dominate its surroundings, should be free-standing where possible, and should only be measured against itself.

Was Körner's synagogue in Essen such a "character building"? The large arched windows with their tracery, the decorative intrados on the gateway, the double and triple windows, most predominantly in the Rabbi's house, the design of the west building with its tympanum, the round window over the gateway and the flanking stairwell towers are equally Romanic architectural forms and elements of church buildings. In the interior, the heightening of the space and the Torah ark – its positioning and vertical construction is utterly comparable to a high altar – corresponded to church designs. The same applied to the position of the organ.

The interior decorations were a contrast in so far as some of them could be designated by scholars as "oriental" and others could be compared to Byzantine art because of the amount of mosaics. But we should not overlook the fact that Jewish symbols were also part of the successful impression and that the mosaic medallions also harked back to antique synagogue ornamentation. We must also take a more differentiated approach to comparisons with church buildings. The circular window in the tympanum displays the Menorah and not roses. Körner moved the staircase towers almost to the rear, and placed the atrium in the foreground. The heightening of the room and the design of the Torah ark also have correlations with a temple or a church building.

Nonetheless this does not alter the fact that synagogues often resembled churches and this was explained by the lack of a "Jewish architectural form". Hence we should now cast a short look at the history of synagogue architecture.

It is not known for sure when the first synagogue was built. The first archaeological evidence goes back to the 3rd century BCE in the Diaspora in Egypt. This was followed by further buildings in the 2nd century BCE in the Mediterranean area and the Near East. The building type could be traced back to an ancient meeting place, the hall in the basilica. This profane architectural form was then adopted and converted to become a Jewish meeting place with a Torah and Torah ark.

Essen, the synagogue, in the past: II. Weberstraße, today: Gerswidastraße/Gänsemarkt, drawing "May 1869" by Bauinspektor Spannagel (City archives, file of the house)

The first synagogues in Germany were built in the 11th century as centres for Jewish settlements along the River Rhine. Mediaeval synagogues resembled church buildings and the repertoire of Western shapes; hence they did not give rise to specific Jewish forms of architecture. In contrast to churches with three aisles, as a rule synagogues only had two: they also had a window over the Torah ark, frequently in the shape of an eye.

In the 17th and early 18th centuries there were further developments: long rectangular buildings gave way to a central room (often on a rectangular ground plan), the Torah ark was placed opposite the entrance, the first women's galleries were built and pairs of windows were set in the east wall.

The Age of Enlightenment witnessed a change in synagogue architecture. As society became more tolerant in its attitudes Jews gradually began to be socially and legally accepted as equals, although this was often hotly debated. Jewish communities grew in the towns and new synagogues were built, no longer in out-of-the-way locations like back yards, but as representative buildings. Finally synagogues in the late 18th and 19th centuries had a variety of concepts and stylistic solutions.

The synagogue in Wörlitz is significant. It was built by Prince Leopold III. Friedrich Franz von Anhalt in 1789 (see Cohen-Mushlin, Aliza u. Thies, Harmen H.

(eds): Synagogenarchitektur in Deutschland, p. 69). This is the first freestanding synagogue in a circular form to be built in a classical style. Its exterior was based on the ancient Roman Vesta Temple and its interior (the inventory was destroyed in 1938) on the Pantheon. The exterior of the circular building was subdivided by 12 pillars and had a range of round windows in the upper zone. The Prince wanted the synagogue to give expression to Enlightenment tolerance. Hence its innovatory design should be a palpable expression, "(...) that an enlightened Jewish culture can have a place in an enlightened world".[13] The reference to ancient Roman buildings pointed back to the long tradition of Jewish culture and religion irrespective of the fact that ancient synagogues had no resemblance whatsoever to that in Wörlitz, a fact that was neither known nor relevant. This was the first round synagogue building and as such it was unique!

After 1800 Jews themselves began to commission synagogues and formulate their own new ideas and concepts. Jewish Enlightenment, the Haskalah, led to decisively different ways of thinking which equally affected their services and synagogues.

The earliest architectural testimony to the Jewish reform movement was the synagogue attached to the Jacobson school in Seesen that opened in 1801. It was built by Israel Jacobson and displayed some fundamentally new features. The bimah no longer stood in the centre of the room but on the east side by the Torah ark; services were held in German and there were also inscriptions in Hebrew and Latin. The three-aisled synagogue had a turret in which there was probably a bell – for a synagogue this was an equally alien element as the organ that was also included in the building. Jacobson wanted the building to be a "general house of God" for monotheistic religions. Knufinke put it aptly when he wrote: "This building should not only show that a synagogue can resemble a church, but also that a church can resemble a synagogue."[14] It was known as "Jacob's Temple" and it is scarcely a surprise that from then on the Torah ark was preferred as an abbreviation of the Jerusalem Temple because Reform Jews placed more importance on living on an equal footing in Germany than the prospect of a return to Jerusalem. The "new Temple" was built in Germany, because: "For these Jews the Holy Land was not simply Palestine as the Zionists declared, but indeed Germany."[15]

Indeed the lives and economic status of many Jews in Germany improved considerably in the course of the 19th century, and this was clear from the construction of new large synagogues. This achievement often went along with assimilation into a Christian society. Sometimes Jews even went so far as to be baptised but this was regarded critically by Jewish communities. The design of the synagogues reveals the thin line between integration and autonomy. They were to become, so to speak, seismographs for the place of Jews in society. Under the premises of being "characteristic", synagogues were given an Oriental style in the broadest sense because it was assumed that the origin of Jewish

Wörlitz, built 1789

The "temple" in Seesen, built 1810.
View to the south-east

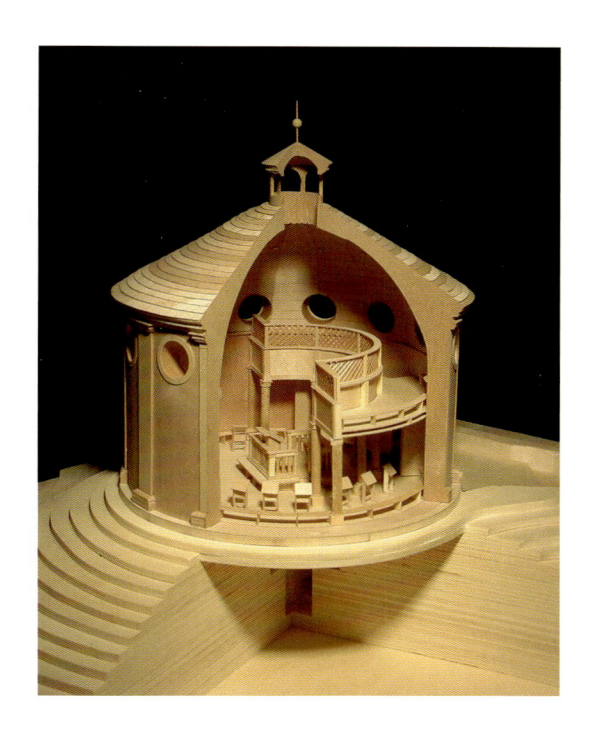

culture and religion was in the East. But some people in urban areas were so disturbed by synagogues featuring Moorish, Islamic and even Egyptian features that they frequently accused Jews of not being willing to adapt to German society. "One of the most common accusations made in debates on the emancipation of the Jews was the charge that they belonged to a foreign `nation'(...)."[16]

Gottfried Semper managed to solve this conflict in so far as he differentiated between the exterior and interior in the synagogue he designed in Dresden in 1840. Rounded arches on the outside harked back to mediaeval Christian architecture whilst the colouring and ornamentation in the interior had a vaguely oriental touch. The Jewish architect Albert Rosengarten preferred the so-called "classicist round arch style" with Romanic elements that was predominant around 1850. A Romanic style was not only meant to establish a reference to Christian churches but also to mediaeval synagogues, and thus to a Jewish tradition in Germany.

There again, Eduard Knoblauch's synagogue that was opened in 1866 in Oranienburger Straße in Berlin was by far the most splendid and largest building in a "Moorish" style. As such it reminded people of the influential age of Jews in Moorish Spain and expressed the autonomy and the acceptance of the Jewish community in Prussian Berlin.

Old Synagogue Essen – House of Jewish Culture

The Jewish architect Edwin Oppler criticised this style because he was thought it would support the suspicion of separatism and hinder the emancipation of the Jews. Referring back to mediaeval synagogues that did not want to be distinguished from Christian buildings, he pleaded in favour of building synagogues in a "German style". By this he understood Romanic-style architecture. Hence his synagogue in Hanover which opened in 1870 represents an attempt to adapt to current building styles.

There was a change in the design of synagogues around 1900. This went along with a general tendency in architecture to discard historicism in favour of new building styles. On the one hand Jugendstil offered an alternative, and on the other hand there was a tendency to simplify forms in order to give buildings a coherent unity. Nonetheless classicist forms continued.

A monumental style began to develop in the late Wilhelmine age. Its bulky massive appearance was supposed to give a building dignity and pathos. Historicism had achieved this effect by quoting dignified historic forms, but now this should be more strongly expressed by its coherence. In the context of the cult of monuments this style was transferred to cemetery buildings, water towers, railway stations, industrial buildings – and of course synagogues.

Henry Hobson Richardson was the main originator of monumental styles in the USA. He had designed several particularly massive buildings in a neo-Romanic style, featuring ornamented embraces, two and three mullioned windows and recessed pillars. Similar features can also be found in the synagogue in Essen.

But not solely in Essen. For in the period before the First World War a huge number of synagogues were built in this monumental style. These included those in Darmstadt in 1906, Poznan and Frankfurt am Main (Friedberger Anlage) in 1907, in Wittlich, Bamberg and once again in Frankfurt am Main (the synagogue in the Westend area) in 1910, in Görlitz in 1911, and in Regensburg, Mainz and Berlin (Fasanenstraße) in 1912.

With regard to the circular main room in the Essen synagogue, similar examples can be found in Mainz (a circular building) and the synagogue in Görlitz (a main room with an almost circular ground plan). The idea for a circular building first showed up in Wilhelm Wellerdick's design for the Frankfurter Westend synagoge in 1907. Körner had also submitted a design for the synagogue. It shows a synagogue with highly rectangular shapes, strongly influenced by Romanic architecture and imposing towers on the west side. We may assume that Körner was acquainted with Wellerdick's design. Indeed this might have inspired his design for the synagogue in Essen. That said, there were very clear differences. For the Jewish community centre in the West End of Frankfurt, Wellerdick designed the prayer room as a circular building, to which he attached rectangular building sections. If we look at the structure of the walls with their pilaster strips and round windows in the upper zone, the circular building itself is reminiscent of the classicist synagogue in Wörlitz. In so far as this design was never realised it was not a benchmark for Körner.

Dresden, The synagogue from the south. Architect Gottfried Semper, 1870

Berlin, Exterior and interior of the synagogue in Oranienburger Straße. 1866, Architect Eduard Knoblauch

Hannover, The synagogue, 1864–1870, Architect Edwin Oppler. View from the south-west

It might be more revealing to look at the building that was realised according to Franz Roeckle's design, especially with regard to the shape of the roof. The synagogue site is on a corner plot and does not have the same symmetry as in Essen. That said it has a very beautiful, rhythmically staggered composition of dynamic, convex roof shapes, a decisive motif that Körner adopted in Essen.

The architect Willy Graf was clearly inspired by Wellerdick's design when he designed the synagogue in Mainz as a circular building with a corresponding exterior structure. We must also take into account that he also planned a comprehensive group of individual buildings for a community centre, thereby finding an additive solution consisting of a central circular building to which further buildings were attached. By contrast, Körner succeeded in designing an overall compact, closed and homogeneous building in which the circular main room is powerfully integrated.

Seen from this angle the synagogue in Essen is rather more comparable with that in Görlitz, designed by the architects Lossow and Kühne (it is still used as a cultural centre and meeting place). Here the almost circular main room is placed in an overall building which, by contrast with that in Essen, rises from a rectangular ground plan and shows elements of antique design. That said, similar to the synagogue in Essen, rounded segments on the exterior of the building reflect the circular shape of the main room. In addition monumentalisation had already been used in Görlitz: a cast iron, eye-catching tower lies on top of the main room, and the dome is placed over a tall hollow space.

Previously the synagogue in Poznan, which opened in 1907, was made higher by two dome shells. These are comparable with Körner's synagogue on the grounds of their rounded building segments and staggered dome roofs. But the synagogue in Poznan lacks a consistent repetition in the form of a forecourt, and the highly specific sculptural shape of the synagogue in Essen, which gives it its imposing, massive character. Hence the following judgement: "In comparison to the other contemporary monumental synagogue building projects the synagogue in Essen is strikingly distinguishable by its conspicuously displayed monumentality as the climax of this development." [17]

The Modern style played a major role in the design of the synagogue in Essen. This was expressed in a modern building construction, the modern style of imagery, the use of motifs by a popular Jugendstil artist and – on top of all the rich decoration – in its Gesamtkunstwerk composition. Last not least, when seen from the point of view of modern design, the commission to make the mosaics and stained-glass paintings were given to Gottfried Heinersdorff and the Puhl & Wagner firm, both of whom were leaders in this area and had a network of contacts with a large number of contemporary artists. The upshot was that this synagogue was, as near as possible, up-to-date and reflected the Jewish community's interest in art and its commitment to culture. In this way it succeeded in building a satisfactory architectural monument that can be seen as the expression

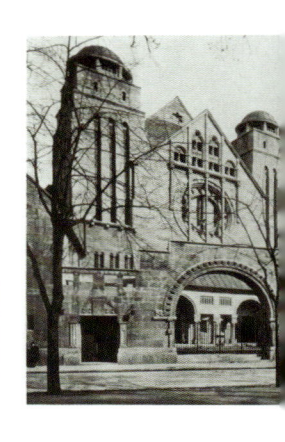

66   The Architecture of the Old Synagogue in Essen. Observations on the historic building

Top row (left to right)

Berlin, The synagogue in Fasanenstraße, 1912. View from the north-west, Architect Ehrenfried Hessel

Regensburg, The synagogue, 1912. Architect Joseph Koch

Frankfurt am Main, The Synagogue Friedberger Anlage, 1907.
   Architects Peter Jürgensen and Jürgen Bachmann. West side

Frankfurt, The Westend Synagogue. 1910. Architect Franz Roeckle

Darmstadt, The orthodox synagogue, 1906. View from the north-west. Architect Georg Wickop

Bottom row

The synagogue in Wittlich, 1910. Current state. Architect Johannes Vienken

Bamberg, The new synagogue, west façade. Architect Johannes Kronfuss

Poznan, The synagogue. View from the south-west. Architects Wilhelm Kremer and Richard Wolffenstein

Poznan, The synagogue, 1907. View from the north-east

Görlitz, The synagogue, 1911. Architects William Lossow and Hans Max Kühne, current state
   (in renovation 2016)

Mainz, The synagogue, 1912. Architect Willi Graf

Old Synagogue Essen – House of Jewish Culture

68 The Architecture of the Old Synagogue in Essen. Observations on the historic building

of its self-affirmation, the cohesiveness of its community and its place within a Christian society. Simultaneously, at a time of palpably increasing anti-Jewish prejudice this "character building" was simultaneously a sign of tolerance and common features with its Christian surroundings and a self-confident contribution to Jewish tradition and Jewish art, a theme that was a matter of broad public debate in the period before the First World War. Hence the following conclusion can be drawn: "(...) Thus priority was given to an inner-Jewish tradition, and there was no value attached to the intensive adaptation efforts during the previous decades, (...)." [18]

Körner's synagogue in Essen proved exemplary. In 1914 the architect Ernst Cohn built a synagogue in Bad Wildungen with a main room on an almost circular ground plan, in which six windows portrayed the six days of creation. The synagogue in Wilhelmshaven that opened in 1915, with its base level ashlar frames, dynamic roof shapes, stained-glass windows and large amount of decorative elements is also definitely comparable. And finally the 1916 synagogue in Offenbach also had a round main room to which a staircase tower was attached in order to give it a more monumental effect (it is used today as a cultural and events centre).

But we can even go further forward in time. In the early 1930s the Jewish community in Essen commissioned Erich Mendelsohn to build a young people's home. It was completely destroyed in 1938. Mendelsohn emigrated to the USA where he was commissioned to build a Jewish community centre in Cleveland, Ohio. The Park synagogue that was built between 1946 and 1953 quotes from Körner's synagogue in Essen, in that it selected a wedge shaped ground plan and spanned the prayer room with a copper dome (see Cobbers, Arnt: Erich Mendelsohn. 1887–1953. Der analytische Visionär, Cologne 2007, p. 86).

In 1959 the post-war Jewish community in Essen had a new synagogue built on the site of the former Young People's Home. The architects responsible were Dieter Knoblauch and Heinz Heise. Their design harked back to Körner and Mendelsohn, for the community centre was built on a triangular ground plan with a circular dome shell in the middle.

Top row from the left
Frankfurt/Main, A design for the Westend synagogue, 1907, Architect Wilhelm Wellerdick

Frankfurt/Main, A design for the Westend synagogue, 1907, Architect Edmund Körner

Bottom row from the left
The interior of the synagogue in Mainz, 1912

The interior of synagogue in Görlitz, looking East

The synagogue in Wilhelmshaven, 1915

The synagogue in Offenbach, 1916

Edmund Körner – one of the leading architects in Essen

Edmund Körner arrived in Essen from Berlin in 1908. What impressions did he have of the city? And how did he regard his work in a city that had grown as a result of industrialisation? In 1912, when the synagogue was being built, Körner wrote: "Anyone who loves a vibrant life, knows how to work creatively in a fresh and happy manner, and wants to get on in life, will soon feel at home in Essen, the city that has no idea what stagnation means". [19] In Essen, Körner had more than enough opportunities to "work creatively", not least because of the huge success of the synagogue which resulted in new commissions, particularly from wealthy Jewish citizens. Hence it was not long before he was regarded as one of the most important architects in the city alongside Alfred Fischer and Georg Metzendorf.

Edmund Körner was born in Leschnitz (a district of Görlitz) in 1874, where he enjoyed a very good education. He completed an apprenticeship as a carpenter and worked as a building technician before he took up a course at the Building Academy in Sulza and visited the Technical University in Dresden. In 1897 he took up a post with the Dresden Tramways and designed the first tram stations for them. In 1906 he passed the Saxon Architects' examination and followed this by working at Johannes Otzen's Berlin atelier for "Mediaeval Architecture with special emphasis on church art". In 1907 he was awarded the "Major State Academic Prize in the area of Architecture".

As well as designing the synagogue in Essen, Körner was responsible for designing the People's School (Volksschule) in Tiegelstraße as early as 1910 (see Pankoke, illustration 13) and also drew the plans for the Building Trade School in 1908. The latter still plays a decisive role in the Moltke quarter as the Robert Schmidt Vocational College. As with his design for the synagogue Körner reworked his initial design for this project to make the building more monumental and give it a tall clock tower, as well as adding a high plinth made of rusticate masonry. Klapheck wrote that the Building Trade School was as equally important as the synagogue in the urban development of the city. And Körner wrote: "When the extension to Moltkestraße has been completed and its projected endpoint is bordered off by a large building, as intended, this will surely result (…) in an impressive urban image." [20] Here we can hear Körner's desire to give the city a new image by means of representative buildings. Thus he remarked: "A large amount of new monumental buildings for Essen is in the planning stage (…). There is a good chance that we shall still be able to achieve impressive, munificent images in the city. [21] In doing so he posited his starting position as such: "To be quite honest the lack of any local building traditions and the totally opaque situation in the area of architecture (…) has led to an utterly grotesque inconsistency in the appearance of the streets." [22]

Just as on his synagogue there are many decorative elements on Körner's School of Applied Arts: reliefs with figures and ornaments on the facade as well as sculptures in front of the entrance. This sort of decoration on a building is one of Körner's trademarks. Especially when working on villas, he could demonstrate his love for comprehensive decorative interior design, and he received much recognition and praise for his colour balance. Good examples here are the villas belonging to the family of the merchant Eugen von Waldthausen at Moltkeplatz and the Jewish merchant Carl Herzberg at Haumannplatz. Both were built in 1911/12 and neither exists any more.

Körner initially used bricks for Carl Herzberg's villa . At first this type of building material was not typical for the region around Essen but because of its resistance to pollution in industrial regions it gradually became generally accepted. Thus it was frequently used by Körner in his future designs, like that of the office of the Jewish solicitor and notary Salomon Heinemann in Zweigert-straße in 1914 (see Pankoke, illustration 40). Körner assembled cubic building structures in such a way that recessed floors had space for balconies and terraces. He softened hard edges by rounding off the corners and here again his preference for rounded building shapes can be recognised. Decorated sections and tondi (round reliefs) with figurative representations can still be seen today on Heinemann's office building.

Körner may have received some ideas, especially for decorative forms, from the Mathildenhöhe in Darmstadt. His post in the artists' colony in August 1911 was probably due to the positive response in expert circles to his synagogue in Essen. For the planned exhibition in Darmstadt Körner designed a number of different pavilions and furnished the Hall of Honour in the exhibition building with mosaics, that were once more executed by the Puhl & Wagner company. The influence of Körner's activities in Darmstadt can be seen in the stone and metal works in the synagogue, for: "Edmund Körner's designs followed the stringent, rhythmic, dynamic forms to be found in Darmstadt Jugendstil." [23]

Körner gave up his post in the City Building Design Department in Essen as early as 1911 in order to go freelance. In the city he worked with other artists and employed them to furnish his buildings. These included Johan Thorn Prikker, Will Lammert and Joseph Enseling who were then working in the Academy of Applied Arts and the artists' colony in Margarethenhöhe. Körner kept his office on the synagogue building site until 1914. He then rented rooms in the "Handelshof" business house before moving to the "Glückaufhaus" office building in 1928. When the latter had to be cleared in 1933 to make room for the Nazi district administration (Gauleitung) in Essen, Körner set up his atelier in the "Baedeker House". During the Nazi period Körner was temporarily forbidden to exercise his profession, probably because he had been responsible for the synagogue and had worked for other Jewish persons or companies. Even when we may assume that this ban was lifted in 1938, Körner received no further commissions. Thus his final design was for a large factory site belonging to the Ford Motor Company in Cologne. In winter 1940 he fell ill with a pulmonary infection and died in Essen in February that year. He was laid to rest in the Park Cemetery, after being forced to witness the desecration of his synagogue.

Since Körner was not called up during the First World War his war service consisted of designing war memorials. For the square in front of the Handelshof – in front of his own office – he designed a pavilion for the "Blacksmith of Essen", a so-called "Nagelstandbild", (a nailed up statue) that could be seen in many German towns at the time. Nailed-up images and statues were used to collect money for widows, orphans and soldiers who had been severely wounded during the war.

In the years of crisis after the First World War, architecture was marked by the search for new forms of expression. This was highly evident in Körner's design for the Essen Exchange. His previous preference for rounded forms now gave way to the reverse; angular shapes. The original tall arcades in the building were supported by octagonal pillars and their arches were angled off at the edges to fall away into a stepped embrasure. The vertical direction of the building was also emphasised by high triple windows and the top of the seven-storey building was strikingly designed to resemble the bow of a ship. Here Körner's building is very similar to the Chile House designed by Franz Höger in Hamburg. The triangular "ship's bow" shape thrusting out into the street was probably influenced by Mies van der Rohe's 1922 "honeycomb" design for a high-rise building in Friedrichstraße in Berlin, with the exception that neither of the two architects imitated his daring steel and glass construction.

The Essen Exchange existed until 1935. It was rebuilt after the war and is now the site of the "Haus der Technik". The rounded arches in the arcades did not suit the original character of the building, but the typical crystalline structure was clear from the alternately projecting and recoiling segments in the facade, which were to be the trade marks in various buildings designed by Körner, for example in the two villas he designed in 1922/23 for Hermann Stern and Willy Cohn.

Part of the Catholic Church of the Holy Guardian Angel in Frillendorf, designed by Körner between 1922 and 1928, also has an innovative zigzag form. It is interesting how similar this is to Körner's initial design for the synagogue. The huge deeply drawn-down cupola of the church with its sharp triangular dormers resembles the dome with its sharp-edged dwarf gables that Körner originally conceived for his synagogue. Both the dome on the church and the synagogue consisted of a twin shell. In the church this is not so much because Körner wanted to give it more height, but rather to subdue the amount of light falling into the building. Körner resolved the ambivalence in his synagogue between a centralised and a directional building, by placing his design for the church on an oval ground plan. A template for an oval central building surrounded by niches can be found in the Church of St. Gereon in Cologne, a building whose origins date back to the 4th century. Körner linked the reminiscences of the classical age with a modern architectural form in a highly original manner.[24]

Körner's private houses on Moltkestraße and the Camillo Sitte Platz were built at the end of the 1920s. He moved into the first with his wife in 1928. It was initially intended to be a private sanatorium, and Körner now created a tower-like upper floor with a surrounding row of windows as a workshop. The whole building was made of individual cubic blocks of different sizes assembled in such a way as to leave open spaces for terraces and balconies. There were no more rounded-off corners. Instead the building consisted of clean forms, orthogonal lines and, last not least, a modern-style flat roof. It was plain to see that Körner had no desire to dispense with ornamentations for he placed decorative reliefs on the red-brick facade and artistically designed bars on the doors and windows.

The plans for the house on Camillo Sitte Platz foresaw a number of peripheral buildings and Körner designed a second smaller house that the childless couple moved into as early as 1930. Here he repeated the basic structure of piled up cubic bricks. Roof terraces and a flat roof were also included, but this time he broke up the red-brick facade with areas of white stucco.

Prominent ledges emphasise the horizontal lines and the individual floors. Indeed Körner patterned his design on the 1924 pavilion designed by Karl Friedrich Schinkel in the Charlottenburg Castle Park in Berlin. This might be somewhat surprising but it does show that Körner was only prepared to adopt the "new sobriety" principles of modern architecture under specific conditions.

One of Körner's most prominent commissions was for the Folkwang Museum, for which an extension to the two villas belonging to Hans and Karl Goldschmidt was planned. Surprisingly, and perhaps also significantly, a row flared up between Körner and the museum director, Ernst Gosebruch, with regard to the interior furnishings. Whereas the latter thought the walls should be designed in a neutral fashion as a background to the artworks, Körner argued in favour of a plaster mosaic. It was probably extremely difficult for him to restrain ideas that had earned him so much praise and recognition in the furnishing and ornamentation of other buildings. Whatever the case, Gosebruch came to the conclusion that the interior of the Folkwang building could only prove a success if his ideas prevailed over those of Körner.

Körner was responsible for designing many more buildings in Essen. These include the buildings on the site of the Helene Amalie colliery in Altenessen and the miners' housing estates in Kaiser Wilhelm Park and on the Bischofswiesen site in the same suburb. Many of his designs were never realised. For example, whilst the synagogue was being conceived Körner was working on a design for Steeler Platz, on which Albert Erbe's Old Catholic Church of Peace was later to be erected. In 1911 he completed a design for a business run by the A. Eick family on a prominent site in the forecourt of the railway station. In 1914 and 1925 Körner entered designs in a competition for a new building for the main post office in

Essen; likewise in 1924 for the redevelopment of Burgplatz. Even the Exchange building was originally embedded in a building plan that envisaged a design for the whole of the east side of the station square.

Körner's part in this comprehensive project shows how ambitious and successful he was in reshaping the face of the city. Körner was well aware of the shortcomings and deficits in the scars left on the city by the "industrial jungle". They presented him not only with a challenge but an opportunity.

Footnotes

1 For the quote in the headline see Klapheck, Richard: Die Synagoge in Essen. ["13. Sonderheft der Architektur des XX. Jahrhunderts", 1914], reprint Essen 1980, p. 1
2 See Hammer-Schenk, Harold: Synagogen in Deutschland. Geschichte einer Baugattung im 19. und 20. Jahrhundert (1780–1933). Teil 1. – Hamburg 1981 [Hamburger Beiträge zur Geschichte der deutschen Juden. Bd. VIII.], p. 486
3 See exhibition catalogue: Stationen jüdischen Lebens. Von der Emanzipation bis zur Gegenwart, Bonn 1990, p. 42
4 Gemmeke, Claudia: Die Alte Synagoge in Essen (1913). [Kunstwissenschaft in der Blauen Eule. Bd. 5], Essen 1990, p. 86
5 Ibid., p. 103
6 See exhibition catalogue: Stationen jüdischen Lebens: von der Emanzipation bis zur Gegenwart. Katalogbuch zur Ausstellung „Stationen jüdischen Lebens" in der Alten Synagoge Essen, Bonn 1990, p. 44
7 Synagogen in Deutschland. Eine virtuelle Rekonstruktion, Bonn 2000, p. 28
8 Samuel, Salomon: Geschichte der Juden in Stadt und Synagogenbezirk Essen. Von der Einverleibung Essens in Preußen (1802) bis zur Errichtung der Synagoge am Steeler Tor (1913). Festschrift zur Weihe der Synagoge, Essen 1913, p. 80
9 Samuel, p. 76
10 Foreword by Edmund Körner, in: Klapheck, Richard, Die Neue Synagoge Essen Ruhr, Berlin 1914.
11 See Archive of the Berlinische Galerie, exchange of letters between Körner and the glass painter Heinersdorff, see Gemmeke, 1990, p.165f., 220
12 Samuel, Geschichte, 1913, p. 73
13 See Ulrich Knufinke – In: Cohen-Mushlin, Aliza a. Thies, Harmen H. (Hg.): Synagogenarchitektur in Deutschland. Dokumentation zur Ausstellung „… und ich wurde ihnen zu einem kleinen Heiligtum …" – Synagogen in Deutschland. (Schriftenreihe der Bet Tfila – Forschungsstelle für jüdische Architektur in Europa, Bd. 5), Petersberg 2008, p. 146
14 Cohen-Mushlin, Synagogenarchitektur in Deutschland, 2008, p. 157
15 Hammer-Schenk, Synagogen, 1981, p. 471
16 Ibid., p. 60
17 Gemmeke, p. 81
18 Hammer-Schenk, Synagogen, 1981, p. 470
19 Körner, Edmund: Essens Stadtbild in künstlerischer Hinsicht, in: Deutschland. Zeitschrift für Heimatkunde u. Heimatliebe Nr. 7, 1912. Sondernummer Essen u. Krupp, p. 402
20 Ibid., p. 406
21 Ibid., p. 404
22 Ibid., p. 403
23 Gemmeke, Claudia – In: Alte Synagoge Essen (Hg.): Verluste. Vom Umgang mit einem Bauwerk, Essen, 1990, p. 13
24 The water tower diagonally opposite the Schutzengelkirche, whose shape thoroughly chimes with it, was built in 1925 solely with the collaboration of Körner

Further reading

Alte Synagoge Essen (Hg.): Architektur – Kultur – Religion. Ein Spaziergang durch die Alte Synagoge, Essen 2006

Alte Synagoge Essen (Hg.): Yesterday a Synagogue – House of Jewish Culture today, Essen 1999

Alte Synagoge Essen (Hg.): Verluste. Vom Umgang mit einem Bauwerk, Essen 1990

Exhibition catalogue: Stationen jüdischen Lebens. Von der Emanzipation bis zur Gegenwart, Bonn 1990

Exhibition catalogue: E. M. Lilien. Jugendstil, Erotik, Zionismus. Oz Almog/Gerhard Milchram (Hg.) Im Auftrag des Jüdischen Museums der Stadt Wien u. des Braunschweigischen Landesmuseums, Wien 1998

Birkmann, Günter u.a.: Bedenke vor wem du stehst. 300 Synagogen und ihre Geschichte in Westfalen und Lippe, Essen 1998

Brocke, Michael (Hg.): Feuer an dein Heiligtum gelegt. Zerstörte Synagogen 1938. Nordrhein-Westfalen. Erarbeitet vom Salomon Ludwig Steinheim-Institut für deutsch-jüdische Geschichte, Bochum 1999

Busch, Wilhelm: Bauten der 20er Jahre an Rhein und Ruhr. Architektur als Ausdrucksmittel. (Beiträge zu den Bau- und Kunstdenkmälern im Rheinland. Bd. 32), Köln 1993

Cohen-Mushlin, Aliza/Thies, Harmen H. (Hg.): Synagogenarchitektur in Deutschland. Dokumentation zur Ausstellung "... und ich wurde ihnen zu einem kleinen Heiligtum ..." – Synagogen in Deutschland. (Schriftenreihe der Bet Tfila – Forschungsstelle für jüdische Architektur in Europa, hg. von Aliza Cohen-Mushlin and Harmen Thies, Bd. 5), Petersberg 2008

Cohen-Mushlin, Aliza/Thies, Harmen H. (ed.s): Jewish Architecture in Europe. [Schriftenreihe der Bet Tfila – Forschungsstelle für jüdische Architektur in Europa, ed. by Aliza Cohen-Mushlin and Harmen Thies, vol. 6], Petersberg 2010

Eschwege, Helmut: Die Synagoge in der deutschen Geschichte, Dresden 1980

Festschrift „Baugewerkeschule 1911". Festschrift zur Einweihung der Königlichen Baugewerke Schule Essen Ruhr, 16. November 1911, Essen 1911

Frauberger, Heinrich: Ausstellung von jüdischen Bauten und Kultusgegenständen für Synagoge und Haus in Abbildungen und Originalen. Veranstaltet von der Gesellschaft zur Erforschung jüdischer Kunstdenkmäler zu Frankfurt/M. Katalog, Düsseldorf 1908

Gemmeke, Claudia: Die Alte Synagoge in Essen (1913). (Kunstwissenschaft in der Blauen Eule. Bd. 5), Essen 1990

Gurlitt, Cornelius: Kirchen, Denkmäler und Bestattungsanlagen, in: Handbuch der Architektur, Teil IV, 8. Halbd., Heft 1, Stuttgart 1906

Hammer-Schenk, Harold: Synagogen in Deutschland. Geschichte einer Baugattung im 19. und 20. Jahrhundert (1780–1933). 2 vols. (Hamburger Beiträge zur Geschichte der deutschen Juden, Bd. VIII.), Hamburg 1981

Klapheck, Richard: Die Synagoge in Essen. („13. Sonderheft der Architektur des XX. Jahrhunderts", 1914), Essen 1980

Klemmer, Klemens: Jüdische Baumeister in Deutschland – Architektur vor der Shoah, Stuttgart 1998

Krinsky, Carol Herselle: Synagogues of Europe: Architecture, History, Meaning, New York/London, 1985

Magall, Miriam: Kleine Geschichte der jüdischen Kunst, Köln 1984

Meek, H. A.: The Synagogue, London 1995

Pankoke, Barbara: Der Essener Architekt Edmund Körner (1874–1940). Leben und Werk, Weimar 1996

Pehnt, Wolfgang: Die Architektur des Expressionismus, 3. Aufl., Ostfidern 1998

Samuel, Salomon: Geschichte der Juden in Stadt und Synagogenbezirk Essen. Von der Einverleibung Essens in Preußen (1802) bis zur Errichtung der Synagoge am Steeler Tor (1913). Festschrift zur Weihe der Synagoge, Essen 1913

Schwarz, Hans-Peter (Hg.): Die Architektur der Synagoge, Stuttgart 1988

Synagogen in Deutschland. Eine virtuelle Rekonstruktion. – Bonn: Kunst- und Ausstellungshalle der Bundesrepublik Deutschland GmbH, 2000

Stähli, Hans-Peter: Antike Synagogenkunst, Stuttgart 1988

Wahrhaftig, Myra: Deutsche jüdische Architekten vor und nach 1933 – Das Lexikon. 500 Biographien. Berlin 2005

Wischnitzer-Bernstein, Rachel: The Architecture of the European Synagogue, Philadelphia 1964

The reconstruction of the Old Synagogue, 2008–2010

Lothar Jeromin

The most recent (2008–2010) conversions in the Old Synagogue would be out of context if we did not look at the preceding chronology of building work and conversions, and above all at the causes and content of the changes, and the circumstances involved.

The preparations for the last building phase between 2007 and 2010 included an analysis of the current building substance and equally comprehensive studies on the load-bearing capacity, the materiality, and the dimension of available building material. Despite the conscientious preparations it so happened that during the work on this – currently final – conversion, a deeper examination of the substance revealed a considerable number of demanding, not to say expensive, surprises. Nonetheless it should also be noted here that the capped construction costs were exactly complied with.

During the preparation for the current conversions there were particular controversies about the existing and newly formulated aims, and the content.

At the start of the 1980s (in terms of content) and in 1986 (as a result of a partial reconstruction) the Old Synagogue was substantively converted into a memorial site.

In the 1990s the work in the Old Synagogue grew and changed in many ways. The building became a meeting place for people of different ages, different interests and motives. Furthermore there was a range of events with utterly different content and character: talks, seminars, symposia, concerts, plays and temporary exhibitions.

With the growing knowledge that this unique building was a former site of Jewish life came the first considerations of how to develop the synagogue building, (along with its historical importance, its memories and commemorations) into a place where people could get to know more about current Jewish culture. This approach was turned into reality with the conversions that took place between 2008 and 2010.

One of the most important guiding principles was formulated early on: the building is the foremost and most important exhibit.

Analysis

Much of the content implemented during the 1980s was clearly related to feelings of guilt about the Holocaust – this also applied to the way the new interior was fitted out and detailed. This entirely chimed with the then aim of turning the synagogue into a place of memorial.

The intention behind reconverting the building away from a place of memorial was grounded in the idea that we should not think of Jews exclusively in the light of their annihilation but rather try to acquaint people with Jewish culture. Exclusive memorials of mass murder can be found in other places like Cologne and Düsseldorf.

These two chronologically staggered aims were diametrically opposite to one another. The question about the "face" of the new conversion led willy-nilly to a hard look at current artistic fashions.

Because there was nothing of any substance worth protecting in the interior, it was not listed. Nothing original remained from the year in which the synagogue was built. The interior was reconstructed to some extent between 1986 and 1988.

Edmund Körner's design was shot through with the attempt to create a total work of art. He designed everything down to the last detail and everything was related to the whole. The whole was clearly more that the sum of its parts.

It was extremely difficult to try to recreate something out of nothing. But even in the 1980s it was impossible to restore the building to its original state. Today, one might even say, no one wanted to do so anyway.

All that remained were the spatial geometrical outlines and their contours.

But what also remained was the then contemporary approach to showing the loss of details as empty white spaces, powerful simplifications of the former rich details and composition. Nowadays such an approach is much rarer.

Renouncing all detailed ornamentation is a form of self-imposed paucity. This might be justified in the case of a memorial site. But in the case of open house for culture it is sadly not enough.

Today, more than a quarter of a century later, architects are challenged by a lot of questions when deciding how to handle the old approaches:

- To replace the rich fountain in the entrance hall with nothing but a half cylindrical niche – which of us will be able to really appreciate the loss if we do not know what was originally there? To replace the richly formed capitals on the columns beneath the women's gallery with nothing but smooth shafts – is this perceptible as a sign of loss? In order to feel a sense of loss we must know what was there beforehand. And anyone without this knowledge will be unable to feel a sense of loss.
- Has not the old approach created its own morphology? A culture of fuzzy imprecision, of almost imperceptible memories? If there is nothing left to grieve about, it is impossible to feel grief
- What is there left for us to interpret from the reshaping of the then new interior? Despite all the previous serious efforts have we been left with nothing but a vague formal image on a less differentiated level, and not the slightest impression of the richly differentiated design of the original interior? The overall design is completely different from the original. Despite all the best endeavours it remains at most schematic.

The women's gallery with pillars, as it was

The current view

It was impossible to correct things to such an extent without taking radical measures. But that would have also meant falsifying the historical facts. So despite all the heavy changes to the substance of the building there was no alternative but to start with the formal status it was given between 1986 and 1988. Accepting this fact meant simultaneously accepting the status of the building as a part of its history. Hence two of the main columns were once more clad in order to cover their previous reinforcements: not with the stone facings that had been lost forever but with plasterboard cladding onto which the stone structure was literally painted in all its artistic details. This may seem somewhat ironic but it is perhaps understandable against the background we have described. We should not try to correct past ideas from a modern perspective, nor should we try to historicise. This is also true for a history that goes back no further than 25 to 30 years. The "expiry date" of some designs can indeed be brief!

Nonetheless a part of the task consisted in treating the designs from the 1980s with respect despite all the easily justifiable criticism of the way the reconstruction was carried out by means of allusions and quotations to what had gone before. Here there were no direct intentions to reconstruct and reproduce matters as can be seen later, for example, in the Church of Our Lady in Dresden or other projects like the City Palace in Berlin. When all is said and done it is still possible to see the interpretative approaches and attitudes inherent in the changes made in the 1980s.

Following the assessment of their inherent architectural quality, one of the decisions made from the knowledge gained from the designs was not to alter the formal impression left by the new conversion. The connection with the original synagogue had already been destroyed at the very latest by the initial conversion in 1960. Thus in the current analysis, the status quo of the interior of the building as it was in the 1980s, was regarded as viable. There was no longer any detailed connection with the original designs. Hence the watchwords were reduction and concentration on spatial aspects, and their transcendental, atmospheric features.

The recognition of the need to reflect something of the richness of the original building threw up further questions. Is there something too schematic about the 1980s reconstruction? Something too "removed" that has produced an almost feeble result? Might it be possible to change this today? But this part of the history of the building also cannot be simply disregarded if the motto is to show that the building is the first and most important exhibit!

The overall design concept meant leaving in place most of what had been found because its quality was a valuable expression of its time, whilst also removing some disruptive features. This provided an opportunity to display and enhance the space as the only available powerful motif, and as a framework for exhibitions.

Hence – even when the temptation was sometimes great – a decision was made not to try to "correct" the substance of the building as it was in the 1980s,

View of the organ as it was (looking from south to east)

to fit in with Körner's original plans. Since this was no longer the original anyway, there should be no effort to add further possibly confusing elements. When it came to completely new structural additions, like the stairway in the south-west stairwell, new designs were turned into reality, but only with great care and in accordance with a minimalist approach. This purely subservient aesthetic was intended to be strictly limited to the essentials – with an occasional and highly conscious humorous wink. Although the tin sheets in the round window in the stairwell still existed, they were deformed. Straightening them up meant that they were now somewhat wavy but this was consciously left as a contrast. Thus the impetus behind the new attempt to reveal the contents shone through in some places, although this was deliberately kept in the background. In this context the way of dealing with the many white spaces which were supposed to highlight the previous rich mosaics in the dome is also clear. After long debates these were quite simply painted over. Thus we can now only get a vague idea of what was originally there. They stand as a silent witness to their origins and to the respective outdated architectural approaches over the years. In the concave space above the Torah shrine they serve a new aim, for they fill its presence and its features with meaning. The depictions on the dome above the Torah shrine are projection surfaces on which to imagine the history of the building. They are a direct reference to the design approaches of the 1980s and simultaneously display a connection with the last areas of mosaic.

Space

The fundamental overall aspect of the magnificent interior of the synagogue was, and is, the composition of its space. Given the assumptions described above, one of the basic aims behind the new design of the building was to highlight the impression of the interior and where possible make it even more impressive.

The space was changed in the 1980s. This resulted in fundamental restrictions in the way it was perceived and on the effect of the light within.

It would have taken a huge amount of technical effort and expense to restore the various changes. Some things simply cannot be changed. Take, for example, the differentiated dramaturgy of the lower level of the dome space, beneath the women's gallery. Here Körner intended the arrangement of the covering of the facade and the building's load-bearing structure to raise the atmosphere in the interior. The pillars supporting the dome stand freely in the room some distance away from the outside walls. They are only connected with the facade via the load-bearing structure of the women's gallery. Thus they make an effective contribution to the spatial composition because their positioning diffuses the rays of light falling into the interior from outside. During the reconstruction made in the 1980s the effect of the refracted light was utterly destroyed by low pilasters which closed the space. Thanks to this artifice – it was not one of Körner's inventions but was already used in mediaeval cathedrals in Europe – the whole area of the building had an insubstantial, bright effect. When the transverse walls were closed the room was broken up into individual niches and felt heavy. Because of problems with the static it was no longer possible to open up the protuberances caused by the reinforced concrete walls. The only remaining possibility of creating a similar impression was by using artificial light from the newly shaped ceiling, at least at darker times of the day.

The aims and thoughts behind Körner's design will be described in great detail at another point. The main theme in this section is the realisation of the design in its constructed form, although we must recognise that the two can never be separated from one another.

The north side of the interior with the women's gallery, as it was

100 years ago

In 1913, the year in which the synagogue was opened, Körner's building was not only modern in terms of its content. In terms of its structural engineering it was also an extremely progressive construction at the time. At first sight this is not immediately recognisable. Nevertheless the comprehensive use of reinforced concrete building sections and constructions has remained substantially important in the building's load-bearing system – even to the present day.

Around 1910 to 1913 the use of reinforced concrete was still in its teething stages, far removed from its general everyday use today. Precise, scientifically proven measurements of the load-bearing behaviour, the tensions and the size of the steel inserts as is usual today were by no means common at the time. Nonetheless, a few architects in Europe achieved distinction at the time, thanks to their courage and their trust in the new technology. How far this went can be seen from the very small dimensions of the different load-bearing sections. Parts of building sections like ceilings spanning relatively large spaces are only 10 cm thick. Nonetheless they can support the live loads that are customary today, even when they were occasionally accidentally perforated – and of course repaired – by demolition hammers during work on the overlying screed. Even the cupolas, of which we shall speak later, are no more than 12 cm thick at their thinnest points. Nowadays these supporting joints would have to be much thicker in order to conform to current building regulations. That said, the Old Synagogue has been standing for more than 100 years. Seen from a construction point of view this has also been due to the rigorous and bold use of the then fledgling principles behind reinforced concrete buildings.

However, as in many buildings from this time, the courage to use new building materials and procedures comes to a halt in the face of visible surfaces, and always before facades. No one could have suspected in advance that a reinforced concrete structure lay behind the natural stone facade. The structure of the two cupolas beneath the green copper roof was also hidden to outside observers. Here too this was backed by an architectural philosophy that was only overhauled by the emerging Modern style that often blatantly displayed the structures of buildings.

Basics

However the Old Synagogue does not purely consist of reinforced concrete. Körner's clever choice of suitable materials and their meaningful and economic application meant that he used a mix of reinforced concrete and masonry construction. Masonry constructions were rigorously used for weighty and load-transferring (vertical) sections, whilst reinforced concrete was used for wide horizontal sections like ceilings, balconies and cupolas. The result was a symbiosis that is still valid in many buildings today.

Beside the general demands on a load-bearing construction, like structural stability and operating efficiency, Körner was faced with the problem of solving two further problems specific to this building.

The first is the sloping topography. Starting from a common point in front of the main entrance to the building, the two streets bordering the site run upwards at an angle to one another. Seen from where they meet, Steeler Straße in the south runs upwards towards the east, at which end it is around 3.50 metres higher. By contrast Alfredistraße drops down by around 1 metre before rising once again further eastwards and beyond the site. The resulting difference in height at the eastern end of the site is almost 4.50 metres, i.e. more than a customary storey higher.

Seen thus, the ground plan of the site is a long triangular area with a slanted surface rising upwards, whereas the surface elevation of the site is crooked. It was therefore imperative for the main storey of the synagogue to be continuously horizontal. The logical reason was that everything beneath this would otherwise have had to be adapted to the different height levels. This was solved by the arrangement of the different functions in the lower floor. The foundation level is therefore neither continuous nor horizontal, but divided into individual terrace-like horizontal part areas. This is reflected in the basement floor level. Here the height offsets are linked by short steps. Körner cleverly chose to place the former weekday synagogue at the eastern end of the site where the room height was greatest. All the rooms and areas arranged above the ground floor level had to correspond to other boundary conditions.

Furthermore Körner was faced with the geophysical demands of the site. Directly adjacent is the old Berne stream. In Körner's time it was confined within a pipe (and still is today), but in earlier times it ran freely through the city creating a boggy area. The loess soil is therefore soft and not very firm, especially on slanting slopes.

Essen, like many parts of the Ruhrgebiet was subject to extreme subsidence as a result of ever-present mining activities. The resulting risks for buildings were well known, and feared. This is why the basic parts of the foundations were made of reinforced concrete. To counterbalance the different levels of subsidence they were linked together by so-called centering beams. The result was a relatively warp-resistant construction whose function was to stabilise the building against subsidence and ground settlement during the building period. The main foundations which conduct the loads from the domes into the ground are up to 3 metres thick in places.

Nonetheless the site suffered massive subsidence and ground settlement. One only has to compare the initial height above sea level at the planning time, with surveys from the present day to see how the site has changed over the past 100 years.

- Height ordinates for the entrance level 1913 = 77.00 above sea level
- Height ordinates for the entrance level 2009 = 73.12 above sea level

As we see today the entrance level of the building is about 3.88 metres below that in 1913. Even when using other surveying methods the sea level as measured here has only minimally changed. Thus ground subsidence on the site and its surroundings has indeed been roughly this amount. Even when we note the fact that some parts of the Ruhrgebiet have witnessed subsidence of well over 10 metres, this is still a significant amount in a period of roughly 50 years. Ground movements must have abated around the middle of the last century when mining activities in the region began to decline.

Thus the building has suffered clearly from the effects of subsidence. Measured by the lateral axis of the dome, the north side is around 44 cm deeper than the south side. The subsidence begins around the longitudinal axis of the dome in a northern direction: it does not run evenly but differs between 2 and 6 cm from east to west. This has resulted in cracks of up to 5 cm in the transverse walls of the two stairwells on the south side and the load-bearing central tower, mainly in the basement. In addition there were cracks in the bracing cross walls in the central axis of the basement, which were carefully filled in during current work on the building. The obliqueness can no longer be seen in the floor, but only in the exterior walls and the window parapets in the interior of the dome. In the 1980s the floors were renovated and made horizontal once more. As a result the window parapets on the south side of the building are roughly 30 cm higher than those on the north side.

Even when running upwards the effects of subsidence are not constant. Whereas the south facade – with minor divergences – is roughly 12 to 20 cm out of sync, the north facade tilts northwards by around 2°. The plumb line deviation is therefore around 3–3.5 cm/m, (i.e. roughly 40 to 50 cm) when measured from the eaves above the large window in the main room. This deviation from the vertical is clearly visible from Alfredistraße, as it is on the Steeler Straße side, particularly in the entrance area to the Rabbi's house. Even at the main entrance to the synagogue it is possible to see that the building clearly inclines towards the north. All the lintels in the three segments above the main entrance have a different height, thereby giving it a saw-toothed impression.

The reinforced concrete domes with their barrel vaults and folding plates are clearly intact and have survived these considerable torsions almost unscathed. True, they are also tilted transversely by around 20 cm but show no signs of cracks or other damage. Their tilt can also be clearly recognised from the distortions near the interior of the dome above the large window. The effect of subsidence was not the same throughout the building because some of the building sections were "weaker" than others. For this reason we may assume that some sections are still under pressure, but have levelled off within the overall context.

That Körner did not rely on the rigidity of a single dome can be seen in the outermost cupola of the building. This dome like building section stands around 12 metres above the interior cupola that can be seen from the room it defines below. The space between the two domes is out of bounds to visitors. The outermost cupola is technically not a pure dome or shell structure. It unites two basically different construction principles: that of a spatial framework and that of a bare cupola shell. The main load-bearing structure in the dome-shaped construction consists of a multitude of several robust, parallel, right-angled intersecting monolithic reinforced concrete frames. Their outside points are joined together by the equally monolithic reinforced concrete shell to make the crosswise frames more rigid. The result is a highly warp-resistant construction – in reality doubled, but in simplified terms statically equivalent to the foundations joined together with centering beams. Pure cupolas are sensitive to irregular subsidence and concentrated loads.

Similar features can be recognised on both the west and east ridge-roof areas above the barrel vaults. These are also thin-walled reinforced concrete structures which are bound at their base with a drawbar ceiling also made of reinforced concrete. Lengthwise the construction is piled up at different heights on several concrete beams. This structure is also very rigid and warp-resistant.

That said, just like the outside dome (in reality a so-called spatial supporting structure), it is based on carpentry techniques using purlins and rafters, but with reinforced concrete. It is not known whether Körner was aware of this overlap or simply aimed at using subsidence-resistant techniques (which wooden support structures lacked to such a degree), but it is very likely. He had indeed completed a course in carpentry at sometime during his studies.

The history of the building and its first conversion

The building was used as a synagogue until 1938. It was left as a burnt-out ruin after it was desecrated by the Nazis. The tracery of the large window was little more than a skeleton, and the seating had been destroyed by fire. The Torah shrine still existed but it had also been distorted by fire damage. The mosaics and other decorations had been destroyed along with the stucco and the cladding around the dome.

The heat of the fire in the lower floor must have been great enough to cause broad structural damage to the images on the concrete ceiling components. The concrete ceiling was split open and the reinforcement bars were laid bare in many places. All the floors on the adjoining Rabbi's house were very heavily damaged.

Both the exterior of the synagogue and the Rabbi's house emerged relatively unscathed from the constantly heavy air raids on Essen, in particular the city centre, during the Second World War.

Thus the interior of the building was associated with massive interventions until 1959 when it was bought by the city of Essen and converted into the House of Industrial Design. Conversion work began at the start of the 1960s. The stone Torah shrine and the women's gallery were completely demolished. A new ceiling including the necessary supports was built at the height of the old women's gallery. A false ceiling was added at the height of the peak of the large window – an extremely complicated structure consisting of half timbered wooden supports rounded off with a light ceiling below. Thus Körner's splendid domed interior was subjected to an equally radical violent mutilation. The dome could no longer be perceived as such from the inside. The south-west stairwell was completely removed and all the others were replaced by new structures.

The entrance area was also newly designed in the style of the time. There was no particular interest in monument protection measures at the time, not even in buildings like the former synagogue. Such brutal interventions in the spatial structure of this major building put the finishing touches on the desecration it suffered in 1938 – but with other means. Thus the last signs of the substance of the interior were thoroughly wiped out, not to speak of the dignity of the building.

This conversion lasted until 1979 when a fire in the interim ceiling to the inner dome put an end to the synagogue's use as an exhibition building.

The second conversion

In 1980 the Old Synagogue was set up as a memorial site and a forum for political and historical documentation. The reconstruction work between 1986 and 1988 left the interior of the former synagogue marginally recognisable once more.

What did this mean for the building in 1986? First of all the building work done in the 1960s had to be removed once more – the ceilings, the supports, the coverings and the staircases. This was no easy undertaking given the dimensions of the previous conversion. Alone the costs of the scaffolding needed to dismantle the intermediate ceiling beneath the dome amounted to more than 370,000 DM at the time.

The false ceiling was removed and the women's gallery was newly constructed in reinforced concrete at roughly the size of the original. The Torah shrine and the neighbouring spaces with the organ gallery were rebuilt in the style of the original plans. The formal version of the new decorations was in complete accordance with the spirit of architecture in the 1980s. Nothing was reconstructed and people were quite satisfied with formally abstract, implicative quotations. The walls were painted in a cool greyish green, whereas the stone cladding and screens were made of shell limestone, partly polished and partly sanded. Additional installations were made whose arrangement and design would be almost inconceivable today. These included a sensible lift for the handicapped, which was unfortunately placed in a prominent position on the women's gallery, and an extension to the women's gallery to the main windows which partially covered them, thereby clearly weakening the impression of the space. Due to the gradation of the women's gallery it was unfavourably reduced to a "leftover area".

The new designs were certainly completed with the best intentions in mind, and with respectable attempts to at least restore the contours of what had been lost. Nonetheless, seen from the present perspective a quarter of a century later, the approach to designing the building should have had completely different guiding principles, not least because of its stated use as a memorial site.

The third conversion

On 27th February 2008 the council of the city of Essen made a unanimous decision to initiate a new concept for the Old Synagogue and turn the building into a cultural meeting place, a house of Jewish culture, with new exhibitions and structural modifications to its interior and the appearance of its immediate environment. In order to realise these aims there had been an architects' competition in 2006 that had been won by "Büro space4" from Stuttgart under the architects Hess and Meyer. However this proved impossible to put into practice on the grounds of cost and for other reasons.

A new concept for the exhibition room and other spaces was then developed in collaboration with the management of the Old Synagogue and its advisors, and the current design was realised according to the following criteria:

– The concept of a clear division between the administration department and the exhibition spaces should be retained. This would be achieved by placing the rooms in the administration department in the basement floor. Until then the administrative department had been on the first level of the West side of the building in the area containing the wardrobes of the women's gallery and the choir.
– Furthermore, functional spaces like larger toilets and cloakrooms should also be placed on the basement floor, along with a larger seminar room for public events, and ancillary rooms, storerooms and staff toilets.
– The whole of the synagogue interior and its adjoining spaces should be reshaped for exhibition purposes and for organising a variety of other socially-orientated uses.

New guidelines for the content were formulated which, in the course of planning, gave rise to the present shape and construction. The aim to re-open the building in time for the European Capital of Culture year 2010 made it necessary to have a planned approach to the construction work (with all its ups and downs).

The main objective was to significantly improve the interior quality of the building. To achieve this, the disturbing features that had been added in the

1980s were removed, and remaining areas were freed of restrictions in order to create a generous, unencumbered space. This enhanced the breadth of the space and emphasised the character of the light. The conversion work proved a great challenge and the work was full of surprises for there were no usable inventory plans.

In short, the plans for the building and its design generated the development and realisation of the following criteria:

- The removal of the separating and restrictive gradation of the women's gallery and its replacement by a generous, coherent exhibition area.
- The removal of the historicising and disruptive system of lights in the dome space and their replacement by a defined new lighting concept to highlight the size of the space in an atmospheric manner.
- The projection of a sequence of images of the synagogue's history on the surface of the dome above the Torah shrine. This is one of the basic self-explanatory components in the building, because the images would speak for themselves and make the synagogue literally "visible" to its visitors.
- Extending the border of the former so-called "singers' gallery" (= the mezzanine) to the periphery of the main room. This would raise the intensity of the spatial experience when viewing one of the high points in the building.
- Linking the different heights in the women's gallery by means of elegant sweeping tiered seating. The stepped seating would remove the previous spatial compartmentalisation and unify it experientially. The differentiated sequence of spaces would arouse interest and make people curious to explore the space.
- Opening up the previously fortress-like, closed entrance doors by means of a transparent, attractive entrance choreography.

Thus the new plans once again complied with Körner's original idea that the whole is more than the sum of its parts. This is where the true value of the improvements in the interior quality of the building can be found. The upshot was a restoration of the unity between form and content, and a rise in its quality.

The technical planning

Functionally speaking the existing building no longer conformed to the regulations. In many areas there were no alternative escape routes and emergency exits and it was extremely difficult for the building to be made barrier-free in even the slightest manner, either for visitors or for those working there. The sanitary facilities were too small and difficult to reach. The cloakrooms scarcely existed, and when they did they were simply insufficient to meet the needs. Furthermore there was no possibility of organising a round tour of the individual areas because these were either substantially separated from one another, or not accessible to the general public.

Hence it was necessary to decide on an overall plan to design the building in such a functional and organisational manner that it would meet all the respective demands made on an open place of assembly.

To do this it was necessary to build a stairway in the south-west stairwell (the previous one had been removed in the 1980s), to build an emergency exit into both stairwells in the ground floor on the west side, and integrate them into the existing facade, as well as to integrate the existing three stairwells and the new one into the system of escape routes. Furthermore it was necessary to ensure that the escape routes were wide enough and to build in a further lift from the basement to the level of the women's gallery, and an additional lift for handicapped people from the women's gallery to the level of the so-called singers' gallery. Finally various doorways had to be cut into the existing walls (they were 1.20 metres thick!) in order to create valid alternative escape routes in all the places on the exhibition levels.

All these measures required a huge amount of complicated work on the building, especially when we consider that they had to be integrated into an exhibition concept that had not yet been thought through.

Furthermore it was imperative to develop a logistics concept to ensure that the day-to-day management of the building and its functions did not get in the way of the building work and that the staff would be able to work in peace during this period.

On top of that it was indispensable to build an extensive ventilation system for the new administration rooms in the basement floor and connect it with the many other rooms in the building that needed ventilating. This also meant having intake and exhaust shafts throughout all the floors and ceilings in the building.

All these measures had to satisfy the strict fire regulations and the almost more stringent security demands on the building, including an extensive alarm system connected to the police alarm system.

The demands on these last two regulations were just as strict during the building period. Indeed they were even complied with when two fire engines arrived in front of the door to check a false alarm from a hidden detector that had not been disconnected.

The preparations

There were many problems that had to be solved before work on the building even began.

On the one hand the building was still surrounded by roads that were used by traffic (Steeler Straße). There was next to no room to set up the building site and prepare all the necessary areas for the equipment. For this reason the right-hand side of Alfredistraße was sealed off and surrounded by fencing during the building period. On the Steeler Straße side the limited amount of room available was also fenced off all the way to the kerbside. The building site fence to the west of the building stretched all the way to Bernestraße, but here the pavement was built out in front of it in order not to endanger passing pedestrians and allow them to reach the Town Hall and the inner city area without interruption.

The right-hand turn from Bernestraße into Alfredistraße was also removed and blocked off. Connections to the building were ensured by two gateways in the fence, one on the south side and the other in Alfredistraße on the north side. Thus enough room was created to set up the necessary transportation and storage areas in the restricted space available.

For security reasons the fencing was made of 2 metre high spruce boards instead of the customary wire mesh. Since the Old Synagogue is designated as a high-security area, the cameras on the synagogue had to be extended to cover the building site area to prevent terrorist attacks or other acts of violence. There were strict entrance controls. Goods transports had to report their arrival in order to ensure that the gates, which were always closed, would be opened.

All these measures created considerable difficulties in ensuring that the work flowed smoothly. Nonetheless the building was completed, as planned, by the middle of 2010 in time for the European Capital of Culture celebrations.

The day-to-day management of the building had to be guaranteed during the building period. The staff entered the building through a security entrance on Alfredistraße. This was also within the fenced-off area and led via the northeast stairwell to the level of the women's gallery, from where the offices over the main entrance could be reached.

The start of building work

Work on the basement floor and its extension to the management level was a task in itself. The north side of this floor was almost on the same level as Alfredistraße, whereas the south side along the Steeler Straße was almost completely beneath ground level. Here the plan was to build rooms for the administrative staff, alongside the necessary toilets for visitors and an adjoining cloakroom. The decreasing space available in the direction of Steeler Straße had to be considerably heightened in order to create the necessary room for the hung ceilings and their technical equipment.

By a stroke of luck, and after closer examination, it was discovered that the side walls of the basement floor on the Steeler Straße side (where the rooms had to be heightened) stretched right down to the newly planned footing base, and even below. Had this not been the case prolonged and expensive measures would have been necessary that would have thrown into question all the plans worked out for this area.

About 1.25 metres of earth had to be dug out from the basement footing – over a total area of 400 m². It goes without saying that such extensive excavation work could not be done by hand. Hence the first task was to open up the outside wall to make space for the necessary machinery. Before that all the natural stone bricks on the exterior facade had to be removed, photographed, numbered and stored away safely. After the work was completed in March 2010 this opening was carefully closed once more. Today it is no longer possible to recognise any traces of this spot, either within or on the outside.

The planned excavation opening was around 2.15 metres wide and 2.75 metres high. Initial excavation work revealed high-voltage cables directly in the path planned for the entrance way. There was no sign of them in the plans and they could not be moved. Hence the final entrance height had to be reduced to 2 metres, just high enough to allow small excavators and earthmovers to squeeze by. This door was given a provisional steel security gate that was only opened during working hours to transport material. This was not the last time that space became scarce because of unforeseen events.

The building access was completed in mid October 2008 and work then began on digging out the earth. Simultaneously demolition work began on the rooms on the north side of the basement floor.

The reinforced concrete interior columns and their foundations in the dug-out basement posed a particular challenge. Their surfaces were only around 40 cm below the existing ground plane. This meant that the ca. 1.50 × 1.50 metre foundations would have protruded through the newly created floor. Since this could not be reconciled with the plans, the concrete ceiling beams above the cellar were provided with heavy-duty props, after which the columns were cut

A dump truck
driving towards the opening

A caterpillar at the
wall opening on the south side

off halfway. The old foundations, each of which weighed around 4½ tons, were removed, dug down deeper and new foundations were concreted. After the concrete on the new foundations had dried, the shafts of the columns which had been removed, could be concreted once again and force-locked to the stumps hanging from the ceiling. Because these supports lay in the main zones of the basement building site, movements in and out of the site had to be restricted for a week for each support. Since all four had to be worked on, this created great time problems.

By spring 2009 all the earth had been excavated from the basement floor (around 980 tons), the walls had been cleaned and sandblasted, and the new soles concreted and grouted. Previously the pipes for the new toilets had been installed and all the surfaces sealed, ready for the subsequent finishing work.

At the same time work was being carried out on the new south-west stairwell adjoining this area. The space here was also confined and the work extremely laborious because all the rubbish and excess mortar from the demolition work on the stairs in the 1960s had been dumped by the stairway stub in the basement. The rubbish had bonded into solid mounds that could only be broken up with demolition hammers and removed by hand because the space was so restricted. In the end, 80 m³ (around 180 tons) of rubbish had to be removed before work on the new stairs could begin.

By this time the new offices on the other side of the floor had already been plastered and furnished, so that the new administrative space was ready for use in summer 2009. The way was now free for the administrative staff, who had defied the dirt and noise by working in the upper floors with a number of electric heaters because the heating system had been removed. They had even been forced to wear gloves on some winter days.

Recurring work

A large number of door-size openings had to be made in the walls in the synagogue basement, some of which were up to 1 metre thick, 1.5 metres wide and 2.20 metres high. To give you an example of the immense amount of work involved in creating such vibration-free openings, of which there were many in the Old Synagogue, I shall now provide a description of a typical operation.

After measuring and sketching out the opening, up to three 200 mm drill holes were made in the wall above the supporting beams. Into each of these a

The new south-west stairwell during construction

steel girder (HEB 100 or 120) was inserted, which protruded from both sides of the wall by between 50 and 80 cm. The girder was inserted on a defined uniform level with the help of wooden crossbeams and heavy-duty props. After that the drill holes (with their girders) were closed up once more by force-locking them to the surrounding wall with mortar. After the mortar had hardened, the props were put on traction to carry the weight of the load-bearing wall. Vertical cuts in the wall were made. The planned opening was drawn and cut on both sides of the wall, depending on its thickness, and on the maximum size and diameter of the saw blade.

A range of overlapping holes around 150 mm in size were then drilled through the brick wall at the height of the lower edge of the cross girder. Thus the weight of the rising wall was transferred onto the ground by the crossbeams and supporting yolks beneath. The cuttings and drillings in the wall produced a rectangle about the size of door opening and this was ultimately broken open with an air hammer. In doing so the vibrations were not transferred to the wall since the section to be broken open had been separated by the cuts from the rest of the wall.

After removing the broken section of the wall, recess supports were placed horizontally into the wall at the height of the headroom, and the steel-profile girders intended to remain over the opening were once more force-locked with mortar. After the mortar had hardened the temporary props were then removed and the cross girders protruding through the wall at the top of the headroom could be cut away with a cutting torch. Finally the outline area and any remaining pieces of wall would be cleaned up with a light air hammer. The result was an opening ready for the next stage of the work, the cladding of the steel girders with fire protection panels.

Because of the large amount of openings to be made, the work was done in cycles, thereby enabling the openings to be made without a break. This was necessary because it took days for the mortar to dry and it made no sense to wait for such a long time because this would have disrupted the tight schedule. The procedure for removing the concrete ceilings will be described in the next chapter.

Here it will become clear that stripping down parts of the building was often more complicated and more expensive than undertaking completely new building measures, which in this case also had to be done.

The upper floors

From the time the administration moved into the new offices in the basement floor in late summer 2009 several projects were being undertaken simultaneously in the upper floors with the initial aim of demolishing and changing the structure of the existing substance in accordance with the demands of the building plan:

- The walls and spatially defining components in the old administrative rooms had to be demolished without replacement before being removed.
- The ceilings in the area allocated for the new lift had to be demolished (ca. 3 × 3 m per floor, through layers of concrete up to 60 cm thick).
- The new south-west stairwell had to be panelled in sections and cemented, as well as being led from the basement to the top floor.
- The huge area of demolition needed for the ventilation system in the two central towers also had to be laid open through the up to 60 cm thick reinforced concrete ceilings covering a total of six levels.

When the walls in the administration area were removed it was discovered that the concreted screed surfaces in the rooms differed by up to 7 cm in height. So it was decided to remove the screed surfaces in the whole area. This was completed bit by bit with a demolition hammer. All in all the work, (including the construction of a new smooth screed surface), took a total of four extra weeks during which no other work could be done in the area.

During this time the lift to take handicapped people one stage higher from the level of the women's gallery was being prepared. As already mentioned, the reinforced concrete ceiling over the whole administrative area is only 10 cm thick. It was therefore not possible to build in a three ton lift without taking extreme measures. But unexpected help came from the fact of the building being on a slope. Since the former floor construction had a thickness of around 25 cm in this area (it had been built especially to compensate for the slope) two solid steel girders could be concealed within the new layer of lightweight screed beneath. Otherwise it would have been impossible to build a lift here. Taking account of the exit on the upper floor – it was impossible to move the position of the lift arbitrarily – the lift for the handicapped was placed almost exactly as planned.

The other new passenger lift was planned to run from the basement to the women's gallery in the south central tower. It was impossible for it to run any higher. Had it done so, it would have broken the contours of the sloping top roof. After the various ceilings have been cut through it became clear that the shaft sloped around 20 cm northwards because the exterior wall was out of sync. Lift constructors customarily work within measurements and tolerances of millimetres. This too was a challenge that could only be overcome by building several extra special constructions.

Looking through the mezzanine

The reconstruction of the Old Synagogue, 2008–2010

The women's gallery

While this work was being carried out plans for the exhibition on other levels were being further developed to make the space on and above the women's gallery as generous and spacious as possible. Thus visitors would be able to experience the area as a whole and there would be more connecting areas for the exhibition. In addition the conversion would restore the original light falling into the room from the large windows.

In the second conversion during the 1980s the original state of the women's gallery was completely recreated, but this time in reinforced concrete. However the floor level was not taken all the way to the outer walls, but given a sort of circular route on a new level in the form of a step around 1 metre high and up to 1.60 metres wide, with an additional ca. 1 metre high concrete balustrade separating it from the rest of the gallery.

As a result the spatial impression left by the six large windows in the lower area of the dome space was badly affected. Furthermore the remaining area within the 2 metre high enclosure felt very restricted and seemed decidedly unsuitable for taking larger exhibitions.

Thus it was decided to take the floor area of the women's gallery all the way to the external walls of the dome space. This meant demolishing the whole of the 1 metre high circular route made of ca. 20 cm thick reinforced concrete and recreating the ceiling openings. In doing this it was vital to ensure that the main columns running through this level of the inner dome were not damaged because this would have led to serious consequences for the stability of the whole building. Careful examinations of the building in the places to be changed showed that there was an additional beam beneath the one-metre slab offset. In addition the studies showed that the system was capable of supporting itself only as a whole. This meant that if the vertical part of the enclosure was removed the remaining part of the joist would have been incapable of supporting the ceiling. This in turn meant that the remaining reinforced concrete beams had to be strengthened in order to be able to carry the new ceiling and its loads.

Consequently heavy steel beams were set under the concrete beams below the women's gallery. Along with the residual load capacity of the concrete beams the weight of the women's gallery could then be transferred onto the neighbouring reinforced concrete columns.

Given the detailed description of the work done along the whole of the women's gallery we can fully appreciate that this was one of the most comprehensive interventions into the substance of the building. Since there were very few drawings of its state it was necessary to make an initial assessment of the load-bearing capacity of the concrete construction. Subsequently the reinforcing elements could be measured. These should not be too high because a new acoustic ceiling had to be placed below the women's gallery. Then again the ceiling should not be so low as to cover the natural stone cladding that had been put on the capitals in the 1980s.

Furthermore the reinforcing elements had to be placed in such a way as to be hidden by the acoustic ceiling and the stone cladding on the columns. This challenge was successfully solved by the planners and the architect.

First the natural stone cladding on the columns on which the reinforcement elements were to be placed was removed in order to survey the load-bearing reinforced concrete columns behind. After it was established that there was no problem here the situation could be exactly measured and calculated. It was necessary to place two HEM 200 steel girders across each working field between the columns. These were 200 millimetres high, and equally wide. They weighed 105 kg pro metre, the equivalent of around 1,500 kg per field, including the connecting structures.

A collar-shaped manchette consisting of 10 to 15 mm thick welded steel plates around 800 mm in length was fixed to the columns beneath the ceiling. This was screwed to the reinforced concrete columns with a precisely calculated number of heavy-duty steel dowels. Thanks to their shear resistance the steel pins on the heavy-duty dowels transferred the complete vertical burden on the reinforcement elements to the columns. Indeed 50 cm thick steel brackets were welded to the steel manchettes to support the load-bearing elements.

After work on all eight bearing points had been completed the supporting elements could be put in place. But first these had to be brought in through the western entrance to the old synagogue. Since each of them was 4 metres in height and weighed around 630 kg this could not be done by hand. Hence they had to be transported up to 40° horizontally on a flatbed truck. In order to make this possible a sturdy wooden horizontal bridge was constructed over the outside steps and all the different levels in the interior. At the decisive points, the main entrance and the entrance hall it left a height of around 1.60 metres, just sufficient for the loads to be taken inside the building. They were lifted into the synagogue with the help of a telescopic crane, and from there by means of steel lifting trucks.

Once inside, the trucks lifted the girders up to the steel brackets lying more than 3 metres above the floor, where they were welded together. Finally the joint between the top edge of the steel beams and the bottom edge of the concrete beams was force-locked with special mortar. After this had hardened demolition work could begin above.

First the 12 cm thick concrete gallery balustrade was cut out by hand into roughly 1 metre vertical segments. After that a horizontal cut was made at the foot of the balustrade to separate each section from the floor. The almost rectangular segments, each of which weighed around 300 kg, were then removed from the building with the aid of hoists and forklift trucks.

Heavy devices needed special ways of transport.

The reconstructed women's gallery received acoustic elements.

Old Synagogue Essen – House of Jewish Culture

106   The reconstruction of the Old Synagogue, 2008–2010

Finally the part of the ceiling due to be removed was cut into segments approximately 1 metre in width. After making a large drill hole in the middle of each segment they were hung beneath a movable cable winch. Subsequently two lengthways cuts were made to separate the segments from the ceiling. The limit stop on the winch ensured that the segment did not drop onto the ground floor, but could be lowered in a controlled fashion before it was taken away. In this way the 18 to 20 individual segments, each of which weighed between 600 and 750 kg were sawn off and removed.

After this it was also planned to use a concrete saw to cut off the protruding parts of the joists. But after removing the screed from these elements it was established that they were, like the screed above them, rounded in form. This made it impossible to use a concrete saw because it could only operate along a straight line. Hence the bottom of the joists was given a series of closely adjoining 200 mm boreholes to quasi separate them from the floor. Vertical cuts were then made into the beams to be removed, and the whole construction removed by an air hammer. The work was extremely arduous and time-consuming. Calculations showed that around 45 tons of reinforced concrete had to be broken up and removed in this way.

Since work on the various spaces in the building was carried out in separate cycles the south side of the gallery could be newly concreted in an identical fashion whilst the other side was being demolished. The area directly adjacent to the floor of the women's gallery had been given a heated screed (roughly 350 m^2) and great care had to be taken not to damage this or it would have had to be replaced completely. Luckily, nothing was damaged. The work on the women's gallery lasted for a total of five months.

The singers' gallery

Extensions to the former administrative areas continued parallel to the work on the women's gallery described above. The so-called singer's gallery above it was the topmost floor of the synagogue alongside other inaccessible areas. After the 1988 conversions it mostly remained unused. The new plans foresaw that this small, but truly "intimate" level could be integrated into the overall exhibition concept. Later the section entitled *History of the Jewish Community* was installed here.

It was extremely difficult to gain access to this level. It could only be reached by a single winding staircase from a small room in front of the former administrative level. After the dividing walls had been demolished, this staircase with a few steps in front could be once again integrated into the building as a defining

Demolishing the plaster boards on the women's gallery

Workers pouring screed onto the women's gallery

A circular saw on the women's gallery

spatial element. The added steps were an invitation for visitors to climb the stairway. A separate lift was added for handicapped persons to reach the gallery-like level.

The singers' gallery is extremely discreet in comparison to the domed main room of the synagogue. Its balustrade is set back only a few metres from the domed part of the room. Nonetheless it leaves a magnificent impression on visitors looking up to it from the domed room below. In order to utilise this level, however, it had to be greatly enlarged. This led to the idea to push forward the balustrade to make it directly adjacent to the domed room, and create several rows of descending steps to make the area a place to stop awhile to savour the whole room within the synagogue.

This meant creating a staircase-like structure covering more than 7.5 metres that would lengthen the singers' gallery by around 3 metres. The construction of steel beams and the like was out of the question. Nonetheless the components had to be incombustible and fire-resistant as well as having to take up the customary weight of visitors moving around the area. So even if the steel supports had been given fire-protection panels they would have been much too heavy to build in over two floors because of their static height and deflection limitations. A structure in the middle, or anywhere else for that matter, was impossible on the grounds that the ceilings were too weak to support it. In addition it would have destroyed the transparency necessary for the Jewish Way of Life section of the exhibition on the level below.

As a result the choice fell on a concrete construction that could meet all the various demands in an elegant fashion:

- The new balustrade level should be about one metre lower than the existing one.
- The difference in height should be bridged by means of a seating row which, for ergonomic reasons, should not exceed the height of 50 cm.
- The concrete section must be large enough to accommodate the necessary reinforcement.
- The new component must be shaped in such a way as to be able to build in the seating row and the necessary linking steps at the right height.
- The various steps should be concreted on top of the finished structure. This component must be made of a single mould in order to reduce the necessary finishing and reinforcement work to a minimum.
- The transverse section must be deflection-resistant in order to avoid deforming the final balustrade at the front.
- The concrete should be pumped in via pipes to its final destination over relatively long distances at reasonable cost and effort.

To accomplish this, the transverse section would be put together from several rectangular blocks. On its lower side it would consist of a 20 cm thick and roughly 1.3 metre broad plate. The middle part (70 cm high and 1.08 metres wide) would be the effective load-bearing section. The connection with the existing ceiling would have an angled profile of 30 respectively 20 mm in thickness and 50 cm in length.

The transverse section was completely made of concrete. Following extensive calculations on the reinforcements its overall shape proved statically effective. The overall area of this section measured 1.22 m². Hence, over a statically necessary length of 8 metres the total weight would be 24.5 tons with an additional visitor load of 500 kg/m² floor area, the equivalent of a further 10 tons maximum load. Thus, in addition to the existing weight of the building, around 17.5 tons had to be led down to the foundations, the equivalent of an additional weight of around fourteen motorcars per side! Such extra loads require careful examinations of the load-bearing walls. To the surprise of all concerned it was established that the walls beneath the new beams consisted solely of two massive columns (clad in plasterboard) with a very thin overlying concrete beam. These were utterly unsuitable to withstand the planned loads.

As a result an intercepting structure was made on each load-bearing side to enable them to take a solid, heavy steel construction in the form of a frame. This was a sort of bridge on which the stepped reinforced concrete beams could rest. The supports for this construction were directly bolted to the directly adjacent surrounding reinforced concrete supports.

Even the shuttering for this component proved a particular challenge. It would have been impossible to transfer the weight of the pumped-in concrete onto the "paper-thin" ceiling above the ground floor without puncturing it. Instead a sturdy construction of wooden beams was stretched across the width of the ground floor from wall to wall on which to place the supports for the shuttering.

The balcony was given two horizontal concrete levels, and the remains of the old balustrade were demolished.

In order to increase the "floating" impression, the new balustrade looking out over the domed space was completely made of glass. The feeling of space is indeed magnificent. Nothing in the balustrade disturbs the view onto all the levels of the domed room and the viewer seems to be a part of that space.

The mezzanine
with visitors

110   The reconstruction of the Old Synagogue, 2008–2010

Upper dome

Dome space

Gallery

Ground floor

Administration

Ground floor

Archive

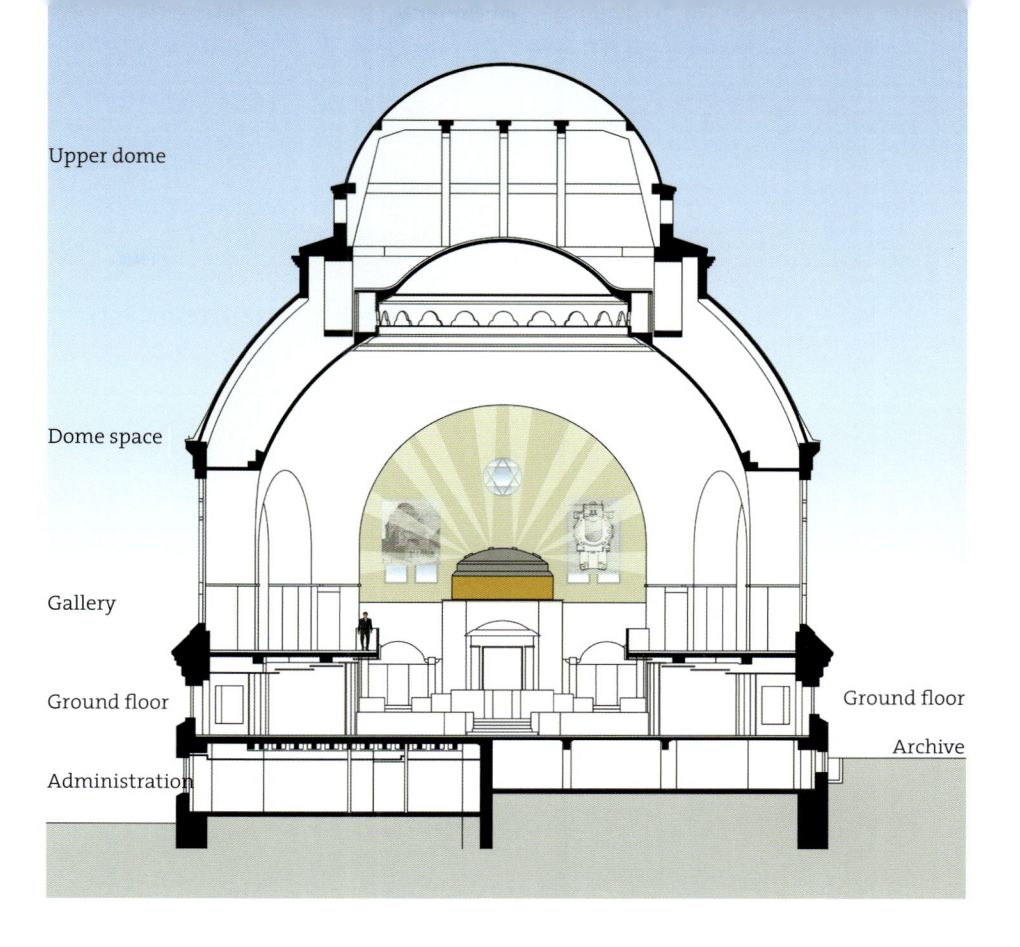

The organ gallery

Opposite the singers' gallery, behind the upper part of the Torah shrine lies the organ gallery that now contains the exhibition section entitled *History of the Building.* In earlier times this level was closed to the general public, also because there was no second escape route. The entrance was by way of a narrow staircase leading from the stairwell on Alfredistraße. In order to remedy the defects in the emergency exits and, above all to enable people to have a connected tour of all the levels in the building, a new second stairway was built in the opposite stairwell on the Steeler Straße side (the south side of the building). This stairwell housed the sole remaining staircase and banisters from the time the synagogue was built. The new connecting staircase is correspondingly modest to suit the tenor of the building. It is made of reinforced concrete and is just wide enough to allow the existing stairway next-door enough room for rescue teams. The Torah shrine and the surrounding components were added in the 1980s.

Architectural drawing

But the most important change to the organ gallery was the inclusion of a total of ninety-six "blank spaces" on the domed ceiling above. This originally contained rich mosaic medallions that had long been lost. During reconstruction work they had been replaced by blank circles, each of which measured 110 cm in diameter.

The idea arose to project a continuous loop of images showing the history of the building onto the blank circles. Special wooden loungers would enable visitors to lie back and view these more comfortably. The images would be projected on the ceiling from high-power beamers set in a copper-clad canopy over the Torah shrine.

The canopy is a 15 cm thick reinforced concrete construction in the form of a cap. Each of the openings through which the images from the beamer are projected is around 80 × 80 cm large. Given the fact that five beamers are necessary and that the canopy itself measures only around 7 × 5 metres in outline, it is easy to imagine that after cutting the holes for the beamers the rest of the construction would be extremely fragile. Hence it had to be strengthened by a steel construction within.

After the holes had been made, steel beams were built onto the bottom side of the canopy on which the beamers were placed. When beamers are in operation they emit a considerable amount of heat which has to be diffused. Additional openings in the concrete would have been so large that nothing would have remained. So it was decided to have a ventilation system for the beamers placed to one side. This is also placed beneath the canopy and is accessible via a hatchway. Thus the space below the canopy is packed with technical equipment.

The projections themselves leave a very strong impression. Like the Northern Lights the images of the history of the building illuminate the ceiling above the Torah shrine even by day, and are immediately noticeable when entering the ground floor of the dome space. "The building is the first and most important exhibit" …

The dome space

After the complicated structural work had been completed precision work could begin in all the areas. The earlier work had produced a thick layer of dust which had to be thoroughly removed, initially in areas which were difficult to reach. The dome space itself – more precisely (and initially) the level of the women's gallery – needed to be redesigned in two places after the demolition of the surrounding narrow raised walkway. The first challenge was the one metre high, now visible bare redbrick wall around the periphery of the area. Secondly, there had previously been an equally one-metre high reinforced concrete step to the former administration rooms, and now a connecting stair had to be put in place to join the two parts of the room.

Even the parts of the shafts of the dome columns to which the concrete beams had been attached, were left bare without any form of cladding.

Where the women's gallery now joins the area holding the *Jewish Way of Life* section of the exhibition a segmented curved staircase with seat steps was built to stretch from the right to the left of the women's gallery in a single sweep. Three sections on top were made accessible by intermediate steps.

The deceptively painted wall cladding

Today the "scars" on the outside walls have a plinth that looks as if it has been made from natural rock but is in fact made of the same shell limestone as the rest of the interior cladding. Its colouring was unique but twenty-five years later it would have be impossible to get hold of the same material in exactly this colouring. Therefore, since the aim was to ensure that the new components strengthened the overall impression of formal unity, a special solution had to be found here. First the plinths beneath the windows in the women's gallery were given thermally insulated plasterboard structures in the desired shape. These were aligned plumb to the sloping exterior walls and therefore had different thicknesses on each side. Glass panels that had been specially painted on the back by stage designers were attached to the substructure. The designers used a "trompe l'oeil" mannerist procedure to give the panels the exact colouring and markings as the existing stone panels. The work was so successful that it was impossible to distinguish the glass panels from the polished natural stone panels, even at second sight.

The same procedure was used on the exposed shafts of the columns, which were made of reinforced concrete clad with natural stone. For structural reasons the remaining space beneath the existing natural stone cladding was so meagre that it was only possible to give it a thin layer of screed. This was then painted over in the style described above. It is almost impossible to recognise any difference between the painted cladding and the natural stone cladding.

So why did we proceed in such a way? This is not easy to answer. We started from the premise that we did not want to add anything new to the changes that had been made in the 1980s that would diverge from the distinctive existing design features. Firstly out of respect for this work, and secondly because the technical problems did not allow the use of new natural stone and we did not wish to destroy the general impression of a new overall totality.

The floor covering on all levels above the ground floor was laid down in exactly the same way, over the floor areas, the steps and seat steps. The reasons for this were both technical and design-related.

After reconstruction work on the women's gallery had been completed in 1988 it was given a carpet over the layer of screed with the underfloor heating. Had we covered it in natural stone or other material it would have been impossible to have an entrance from the stairwells at the same level as the gallery because this would have created a significant ledge. It was impossible to remove the underfloor heating because it had already been reduced to a minimum and there was no space for any additional building measures.

Finally the aim of making all the public areas recognisable by mean of their design, and then linking them together, led to the decision to use a material that was suitable for both vertical and horizontal areas. After intensive preparation the floors were given only a paper-thin covering of fine concrete, which was then polished and oiled after it had hardened in order to give the area a unified appearance. Because of its workable qualities this material was also used on the vertical areas of the seat steps, the stairs and other areas in order to attain the unified impression desired. There were next to no limits to the colours of the material, so the floors could also be integrated into the overall colour concept.

But before work on the floor covering began – this was really the finishing touch – it was necessary to tackle the huge task of cleaning up the surface of the dome and all its adjacent spaces and giving them a new layer of screed. To do this a huge amount of preparation was required. First there were intensive discussions with all those concerned about what colours were to be used. Only then could the dome and the adjacent barrel vaults be scaffolded.

The whole area covered more than 12,000 m^3 (the equivalent of around 15 single-family homes) and the highest point of the dome was exactly 25 metres above the ground. It was therefore decided to place the final working area – a mobile scaffolding – at a height of 20 metres above the ground. From here it would be possible to work on the final 5 metres.

Given the size and the task involved the only solution was to use birdcage scaffolding. As a result the whole space was filled with a 3 × 3 × 3 m. grid of scaffolding that receded when it reached the dome areas. Here circumferential working platforms were placed at a distance of around 2.50 metres from one another. A stairway was constructed in the middle of the scaffolding to enable the workers to reach all the levels.

The scaffolding was almost a building in itself, for it had to be independently designed, constructed, calculated and officially approved. It took four weeks to construct. The necessary steel pipes, links and running boards, ladders and safety barriers were brought into the building via the very same ramp that was used to bring in the transfer beams to the women's gallery. The scaffolding was completed at the end of 2009 so that painting work could begin at the start of 2010. It took three weeks to paint the dome and another three weeks to dismantle and remove the scaffolding. Prior to this all the work at the top of the room also had to be completed; for example, lighting units had to be attached beneath the tambour of the cupola from the top working level of the scaffolding. Had any detail been left out, it would have been impossible to return to it after the scaffolding had been removed. It would have been impossible to work on any area higher than 9 metres above the ground without constructing a secure scaffolding once more. Mobile scaffolding only stretches to a height of up to 9 metres. Above this the scaffolding has to be more massive and stationary. Such "reworking" was inconceivable for financial reasons alone. The same was also true for the time plan. Nonetheless one place had to be re-worked. Not because anything had been forgotten, but because a water pipe between the two domes shells sprung a leak after heavy frost in January 2010. The leaking water caused some damage to the freshly painted interior of the dome. Luckily the damage was within the 9 metre limit so that it could be painted over, albeit at some effort and expense.
Just another of the many surprises that occurred during the conversion work!

The scaffolding was also used to dismantle the large lighting ring and its disruptive mountings in the dome at the height of the women's gallery. This was an abstract reconstruction of the original that was also included during work in the 1980s. Following the decision to open up the building in a generous manner this lighting – it was not the original lighting anyway – was removed after more than twenty-five years. The lighting ring had a diameter of almost 11 metres and like its predecessor was hung from the dome shell. Its position blocked the view from one side of the women's gallery to the other. This could not be radically changed. The lighting ring could be pulled back a little by steel ropes but this was only possible to a maximum height of around 2.50 metres above the ground. Long ladders were used to change the bulbs during use.

In order to dismantle the ca. 500 kg lighting ring the birdcage scaffolding was first erected to a height of 3 metres after which the lighting ring was placed upon it. It was then cut into sections and taken apart. The components were subsequently put into storage.

The wish arose to paint the interior in a cheerful manner. After long controversial debates it was decided to paint the individual areas in different colours (even when they were spatially close to one another) in order to distinguish them from one another. This should highlight the philosophy of diversity over against the common linking unified floor covering.

The upshot was that the whole of the dome space was painted in a consciously serene apricot, the window vaults somewhat darker, the spherical cap at the highest point of the dome in a contrapuntal sky blue, the neighbouring area holding the *Jewish Way of Life* section in classical light green, and the exhibition section *Sources of Jewish Traditions* in a delicate light blue.

A new stairwell

During the conversion to a House of Industrial Design in the 1960s the staircase up to the women's gallery had been closed off and the stairs demolished. During the conversion in the 1980s they were replaced by a small library in the ground floor and the management office in the upper floor. The space in the cellar was filled with rubble and walled up.

Building regulations and museum requirements now made it necessary to activate this stairwell once again. To do this the reinforced concrete ceilings that had been inserted during the 1980 conversion had to be removed and a new stairwell built to link the basement with the ground floor and upper floor.

Thus the architects reverted to the original stairwell in order to be able to build in successively a double flight of winding staircases made of reinforced

The new stairwell on the west side

concrete. After the staircase shell was completed the uppermost hanging wire plaster ceiling could once more be reached and also removed. To everyone's surprise this revealed the original smoke-blackened ceiling (including the surrounding ledges and friezes) from the time the building was built. True, they were partially damaged but all in all they had survived quite well. This ceiling, which was also revealed when the plaster ceiling in the north stairwell was demolished, was integrated into the overall concept of the building as the first and most important exhibit. Two small pieces of the original substance were cleaned up and restored with a layer of glazing and can now be seen in the interior of the building that is otherwise no longer in its original state. Here too, in order to bear witness to the history of the synagogue two rectangles, each the size of a classical cubit (or pechys) were left in the soot-covered state they were in after the desecration in 1938.

Immense discretion was used in the design of the new stairwell. The floor and the steps were constructed with shell limestone panels closely resembling the original material. The banisters and handrails were reduced to their basic functions, although they do display a recognisable form during their course. The surrounding walls are plain white. The aim behind the design was to create an atmosphere of cool discretion, to underline the dignity of the building, whilst indicating – on a minimal scale – its own independent design.

The two west stairways are also used as emergency exits. Building regulations require them to guarantee a direct path to the outside of the building. This path was initially non-existent. The uncompleted 1950s forecourt offered an access to the two stairwells around halfway between the outside site and the ground floor. However these access paths had been walled up and clad with natural stone plates on the exterior. Hence this seemed to be the ideal place for the required emergency exits.

The problem was that two new relatively large doorways for the emergency exits would have been created on the prominent open west facade (now without a forecourt). In design terms these would have been strikingly prominent and competed with the doorways to the main entrance.

The solution was to link the necessity for information about the building with the technical use of the doors. The emergency doors – they are also incidentally the main doors for the fire services – are designed in the form of high glass cases in which information about the building and its events can be presented. The natural stone intersections and the doorframes are clad in metal whose colour matches the surrounding natural stone. Hence nothing other than the information areas can be seen. This "camouflage" hides the emergency doors which can only be accessed from within. There the doors with their closed screens and corresponding instructions can be clearly recognised as such.

The bronze entrance doors

The exterior of the building as a centre of Jewish culture should have an inviting character. Where else should this be made clear than in the entrance doors? Originally the three twin entrance doors were made of bronze plates with reliefs on the surface. These have now been lost for good. The replacements, dating back to the 1980s, were also cast in bronze. But they had a heavy, closed-off, colossal, inhospitable appearance.

Designing the site in an attractive manner also has a signal effect. Hence, the bronze plates with their reliefs were removed from the heavy door wings and positioned independently in front of the new transparent glass doors like folding shutters. When the Old Synagogue is open to visitors the open shutters look like open doors, thereby signalling that the building is open. The visible glass entrance doors behind them allow visitors to glimpse the first part of the foyer. They open automatically on approach, thereby connecting the exterior of the building with the interior.

When the Old Synagogue is closed the shutters are also closed. Their "heavy" effect is softened by turning them into a setting in front of the glass doors.

Exterior sites

The exterior sites are a basic part of the urban surroundings. As such they had to provide a suitably generous amount of space alongside the building. To achieve this, the previously existing Steeler Straße was foreshortened. The result was that the group of buildings and urban elements around the new square – it bears the name of the architect of the Old Synagogue, Edmund Körner – now constitutes a generous experiential ensemble, especially with the Old Catholic Church of Peace and the re-located Centennial Fountain that has also been repaired.

The large entrance stairway in front of the western facade was designed in a free flowing manner. Until 2009 there was there was a stone sarcophagus on an intermediate platform to remind people of the victims of the Holocaust. Following the new design of the exterior site it was moved to the synagogue garden between the Old Synagogue and the Rabbi's house in order to create a more generous approach to the main entrance.

The Rabbi's house

The function of the Rabbi's House directly adjacent to the synagogue was also radically changed during conversion work. The Jewish community had used it as a temporary meeting place after the war, but after the new synagogue at Sedanplatz was completed the city archives moved into the building around 1960. Since it had been heavily damaged by the fire in 1938 it was in need of a thorough overhaul.

The extremely delicate floor and ceiling constructions were given ribbed slabs: i.e. slender reinforced concrete joists were fitted together at a distance of 60 cm from one another beneath the ceiling plates and built into the floor. A ca. 20 cm thick reinforced bar was then fixed with concrete into the underside of each joist. Because the girder cross-sections were so slender and the concrete coating over the floors was extremely thin – this was normal for the time – the heat of the fire had split almost all the girders on every floor of the building. The reinforcement bars had been laid bare and were corroded. The building was neither suitable for normal use nor for archive areas with a load of up to 1.200 kg/m².

The repairs that took place in the 1960s had been extremely pragmatic. The heavily damaged ceilings were given supports and used as a shell for new concrete ceilings made of stable reinforced concrete. In order for people to be able to reach the upper floors of the building the main staircase was renovated to fit in with the changed geometrical conditions. As a result the now superfluous original ceiling was concealed beneath a hung wire plaster ceiling that was customary at the time.

After the building had been restructured the different floors were arranged between the load-bearing walls so as to be able to meet the needs of the city archives. Here too any reminders of the original use of the building were completely disregarded. Thus the former mikveh, the ritual immersion bath in the lower floor, might also have been lost during this phase of conversion. During repairs in 2011 intensive efforts were made to find it once more, but nothing was found apart from a few small remaining pieces of the wall.

During this time the city archive moved into the new building in the Luisen school. Thus the way was free for a thorough overhaul. Nothing substantial had been changed since the 1961 conversion. Here it was clear that it neither complied with current building laws, nor were its function and energy aspects suitable to satisfy prevailing needs.

As a result the building was stripped of all its unnecessary components right down to the purely structural substance. The roof had to be re-tiled and the attic made suitable for use once more.

The building was intended to be used institutionally. It seemed impossible to join five floors with a single narrow staircase. As a result the ground plans were designed in such a way as to ensure that a large lift – it had to be suitable for handicapped persons – could travel to every floor between the cellar and the attic.

The complete electrical system was modernised and all the single-glazed, wood framed windows were exchanged for double-glazed aluminium windows in agreement with the historic buildings authority. New sanitation facilities were built, ventilation systems constructed and radiators prescribed.

Today the interior of the Rabbi's house is a modern efficient building housing two independent institutes from the University of Duisburg-Essen. One is for health economy; and the other for research on Jewish studies, notably on Hebrew tombstone inscriptions, contains a remarkable 35,000-volume scientific library. It is named after the Jewish philosopher, Salomon Ludwig Steinheim.

Today the redesigned Old Synagogue, the Centennial Fountain, the Old Catholic Church of Peace and the Rabbi's house once again constitute an outstanding urban ensemble that is as prominent in the centre of Essen as at it originally was.

The Exhibits in the
Permanent Exhibition
at the Old Synagogue

Uri R. Kaufmann

The synagogue is sited on a slope leading down to the former Berne stream. This explains why the architect Edmund Körner (1874–1940) had to design steps so as to be able to create a longer horizontal area. The high cupola was intended to be a clear external symbol of the Jewish religious community in the centre of the city. The building was opened on 25th September 1913 and used as a synagogue for the next 25 years until 9th November 1938. After 1919 the present day seminar room served as a weekday synagogue for Eastern European and German Jews: here they could presumably uphold their Orthodox liturgy based on Eastern European melodies, and maintain their particular traditional Hebrew pronunciation. The inclusion of a "prayer community" in the new building may be interpreted as a sign of integration, because the "Betstibel" that were mostly used by Eastern Jews were not integrated into synagogues and communities in many other cities.

On the night of the 9th to 10th November 1938 the interior of the building was destroyed, the Torah scrolls burnt and the organ stolen. After 1940 the cellar in the building was used as an air raid shelter. The building would have suffered even greater destruction were it not for the fact that it was a modern reinforced concrete construction with a twin dome. The incumbent Lord Mayor, a member of the Nazi party, decided not to demolish it completely because of the expense involved.

In 1945 the fire damaged ruin was put under trust management. The Jewish Trust Corporation in the English occupational zone and the post-war religious community asserted a claim to the site. In 1946 Eastern European stateless Jews erected a Sukkah in the synagogue ruins, presumably to mark the survivors' claim to the site. After 1947/48 the rabbi's house, which had not been damaged so heavily, was used by the new post-war Jewish community as a refuge.

In 1959 a new synagogue was built on the site of the former young people's home in Sedanstraße (it had been designed by the famous architect Erich Mendelssohn). In 1959/60 the city bought up the Old Synagogue from the Jewish Trust Corporation and began renovations. In doing so mosaics were chipped off, the remains of paintings removed, the Torah ark dismantled and the women's gallery taken down. A house for industrial design was constructed and the interior rebuilt. A new ceiling concealed the view of the cupola.

Overview

Sections of the permanent exhibition

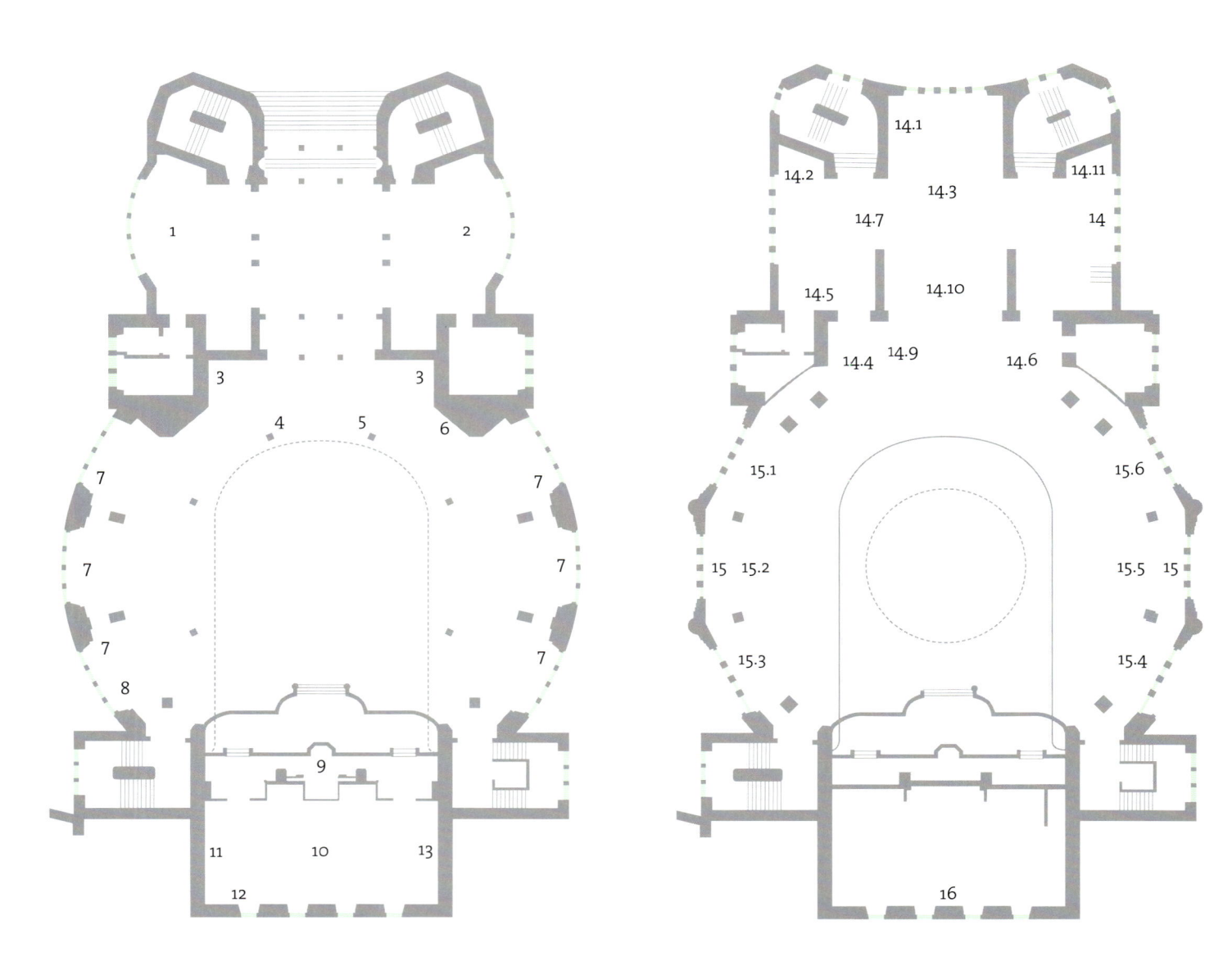

Ground Floor

First Floor

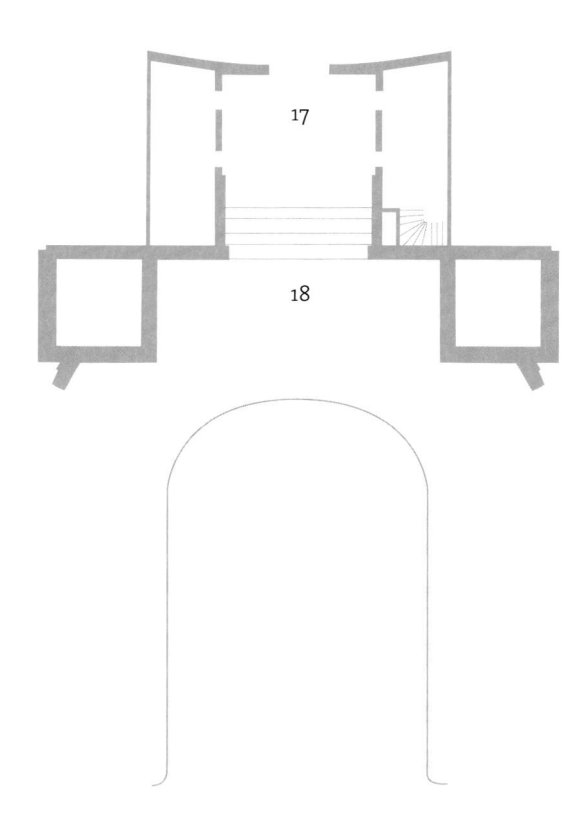

Mezzanine Floor

Exhibits:

1	Reception
2	Café with Jewish newspapers and a monthly magazine
3	Installation: synagogues world wide
4	Wooden model of the Essen synagogue with historical furniture
5	Wooden model of the 18th century traditional baroque synagogue of Halberstadt
6	Map of Jewish communities in today's North Rhine-Westphalia until 1938
7	Historical photographs of the interior
8	Four memorial books for murdered Essen Jews
9	Empty ark of the Torah scrolls
10	Section: *Sources of Jewish Traditions*
11	Chronology of Jewish history
12	Portraits and biographies of Jewish history
13	Jewish and Christian calendars
14	Section: *Jewish Way of Life*
14.1	Literature
14.2	Music
14.3	Folk dance
14.4	Language
14.5	Clothing, personal accessoires
14.6	Films on Jewish identity
14.7	Kashruth: Jewish dietary laws
14.8	Cultural life
14.9	Sports and self-defence
14.10	Touch-table: ten Jewish communities world wide
14.11	Interviews
15	Section: *Jewish Holidays and Shabbat*
15.1	Shabbat
15.2	Purim
15.3	Pessach/Shavuot
15.4	Rosh ha-Shanah/Yom Kippur
15.5	Sukkoth
15.6	Hanukkah
16	Section: *History of the Building*
17	Section: *History of the Jewish Community in Essen*
18	Rest area

Old Synagogue Essen – House of Jewish Culture

Following a cable fire a memorial site was set up in 1979. This was followed by a new plan to redevelop the building in stages. In 1986 large parts of the organ gallery and the Torah ark were reconstructed, and the entrance floor removed. German-Jewish history was presented in a new exhibition and, after 2001, demands were made for an entirely new concept as a house of Jewish culture. This concept was realised and completed with the current permanent exhibition in July 2011 (see the article on the new concept on pages 6–31).

Following the introduction, the current permanent exhibition can be sub-divided into five main areas dealing with the history and function of a synagogue:

1. Sources of Jewish Traditions

2. Jewish Holidays and Shabbat

3. Jewish Way of Life

4. History of the Jewish Community in Essen

5. History of the Building

Entree

Photo installation: What is a Synagogue?

Inscription:

SYNAGOGUE
The word "synagogue" is derived from the Greek word for "bringing together, congregating". The Hebrew term, "Bejt Knesset", also means "House of Congregation". Here Jews gather to study, celebrate, pray and regulate their community affairs.

In the Diaspora the synagogue is the centre of Jewish life and Jewish culture. By contrast with a Christian church a synagogue is not a sacred place. To turn a space into a synagogue requires only the presence of a Torah scroll. Since there are very few architectural parameters synagogue buildings differ from one another according to the time they were built, their region, the political situation in the specific country, the size of the location and the religious perceptions held by each particular community.

The first synagogues were built after the destruction of the First Jerusalem Temple in the 6th century BCE: they continue to exist during the time of the Second Temple that was destroyed by Roman legions in 70 CE. This marked the end of the Temple Cult, which was primarily a sacrificial cult. From now on synagogues were to be the centres of Jewish communities.

TORAH SHRINE
In the First Jerusalem Temple the stone tablets with the Ten Commandments (the Decalogue), were kept in the Ark of the Covenant. Accordingly the Torah shrine is also known as Aron Kodesh, the Sacred Ark. This is where the handwritten Torah scrolls containing the Hebrew texts of the five books of Moses are kept. The Torah shrine in European synagogues can be found on the east wall facing Jerusalem. Even the synagogues in Europe tend to face eastwards in the direction of Jerusalem.

ETERNAL LIGHT
Another reminder of the Temple in Jerusalem is the Eternal Light, Ner Tamid. In the temple this was the Menorah, the seven-branched candleholder. In synagogues Ner Tamid is mostly a lamp hanging near the Torah shrine.

BIMAH
Traditional synagogues also contain a bimah (also known as an almemar or tevah), an elevated platform with a lectern. This is where the excerpts from the Torah scrolls are read out. Over the years various different traditions have developed as to where the Bimah is situated.

WOMEN'S GALLERY
In traditional synagogues the men and women sit in separate places. In mediaeval synagogues there were often annexes or rooms where the women could follow the service. In very Orthodox synagogues it is customary to screen off the prayer room with a curtain, a lattice or a partition wall. By contrast, in liberal and conservative synagogues – say, in the USA – the men and women sit together.

The installation is placed on each side of the immediate entrance to the main room of the synagogue. It shows the diversity of the different architectural styles. Jewish groups adopted the styles in their neighbourhood, but the internal structure was different. In traditional synagogues readings from the Torah scrolls, the five books of Moses, took place in the centre of the building. By contrast Sephardic Jews (i.e. Jews with a Spanish/Islamic tradition who mainly lived in North Africa and the Near East) and Italian Jews read from a raised lectern in the western part of the prayer room. In the 19th century, above all in German-speaking countries, readings were moved to the eastern side of the synagogue. This is how Edmund Körner designed the Essen synagogue in 1913.

1. Ten photos of synagogues in stainless steel frames, 55.4 × 60.5 cm. Design: Jörg Steiner, Wuppertal/Berlin, 2010,
   Located on the north side of the entrance (on the left when facing the Torah ark): Djerba (1920), London (1701), Venice (1525), Piatra Neamt/Romania (1766), Worms (1174/1959),

   Located on the south side of the entrance (on the right when facing the Torah ark): New York (1897), Mumbai (1884), Budapest (1859), Amsterdam (1675), Budapest (1859), Jerusalem (2000).

The south (left) half of the installation showing synagogues from Jerusalem, Amsterdam, Budapest, Mumbai (Bombay) and New York

The north (right) half: Djerba, London, Venice, Piatra Neamt/Romania, Worms

Old Synagogue Essen – House of Jewish Culture

Djerba, Tunisia:

Opened: 1920
Architect: unknown
Seating capacity: unknown

Al Ghriba (The Wondrous, the Strange) is regarded as the oldest synagogue in North Africa. The current building was erected on the foundations of the original building which, according to legend, dates back to 6 BCE. The first synagogue is claimed to have been built by priests from the Jerusalem Temple who escaped after Jerusalem was conquered by the Babylonians in 586 BCE. The main room is surrounded by a low surrounding arcade passage with horseshoe arches.

The high wooden Torah shrine which contains the oldest Torah scroll in the world is situated below the colourfully decorated upper floor. The use of blue tiles with a floral decor is characteristic of the arts in the region.

El Ghriba is a much loved place of pilgrimage for Jews all over the world, who gather there in their thousands to celebrate Lag baOmer (the 33rd day after Passover according to the Sefira).

On 11th April 2002 there was a terrorist attack on the El Ghriba synagogue. A truck filled with liquid gas rammed the synagogue and exploded. 21 people died (including 14 tourists from Germany) and many others were wounded. Al Qaeda claimed responsibility for the deed.

Further reading:
Paul Sebag, Histoire des Juifs de Tunisie, 1995

G. Memmi, Une île en Méditerranée, 1994

G. Memmi, Les Juifs de Djerba: 25 siècles d`histoire, 1990

"Djerba", in: Encyclopaedia Judaica (=EJ) (Detroit 2007), vol. 5, p. 722 f.

"Tunisia", in: EJ, vol. 20, pp. 175–191, see also the bibliography p. 191

Historical note:
Jews lived in Tunisia before the arrival of Islam and the spread of Arabic languages. In the Middle Ages some of them settled in Sicily where they cultivated indigo plants, henna and palms. In the modern era they traded with Malta and Italy. In the 19th and 20th century there were Talmudic Academies in Djerba until it was occupied by Field Marshal Rommel's army during the Second World War in 1943. The Jews were then persecuted and some of them murdered.

In 1945 there were 4,900 Jews living in Djerba. By 1993 this number had sunk to 670. Many of them emigrated to France and Israel. There were attacks on the synagogue or individual Jews in 1978, 1982 and 1985. In the 1990s the Tunisian government adopted a policy of attracting Jewish tourists to Djerba.

London, Great Britain:

Opened: 1701
Architect: Joseph Avis
Seating capacity: 600

The Bevis Marks synagogue is the oldest synagogue in England. For more than a century it was the religious centre of the Anglo-Jewish world. According to legend, timber from a royal ship was built into the roof truss in honour of Queen Anne (1665–1714). With the exception of the roof that was destroyed by fire in 1738 and repaired in 1749, the building still exists in its original state. The exterior of the synagogue is typical of English building styles of the time. By contrast the interior design reflects the influence of the Portuguese synagogue in Amsterdam (1675). Just as in Amsterdam the Torah shrine is on the east wall and the bimah on the west wall, a characteristic of Sephardic synagogues.

In 1992 and 1993 the synagogue was heavily damaged by bomb attacks in London. Repairs were made possible, thanks to a major fundraising campaign.

Further reading:
"London", in: Encyclopaedia Judaica (Detroit 2007), vol. 13, pp. 179–184 (Post-war Period, pp. 182–184)

J. Gould/S. Esh: Jews in Modern Britain, 1964

Historical note:

In 1655, under Oliver Cromwell, Jews were permitted to settle once again in London where they bought up a cemetery site. They had been banished from the kingdom in 1291. In the 17th century Sephardic (i.e. of Spanish origin), long-distance traders were particularly interested in settling in the trading metropolis. It was not long before the Sephardic Jews outnumbered the Ashkenazi Jews from central Europe.

After 1881 many East European Jews emigrated to the East End of London, and elsewhere in the United Kingdom. In 1970 there were estimated to be around 280,000 Jews in London: by 2002 this number had declined to around 195,000 due to emigration and an ageing population.

Even though the Sephardic community in London is small, services still take place in the synagogue.

Venice, Italy:

Opened: 1528/1529
Restored: 1890–1910

The "Scuola Grande Tedesca" was built by the Ashkenazi community. It is the oldest synagogue in the Ghetto Nuovo in Venice. By contrast with the unadorned exterior the interior of the Renaissance building is splendidly adorned with artistically carved woodwork, marble and a huge amount of gilded decorative elements. The text of the Decalogue (the Ten Commandments) runs along a frieze beneath the women's gallery. Thanks to the elliptical women's gallery, the rich décor, and the placing of the Torah shrine and bimah on the two narrow sides of the room, the highly asymmetrical trapezoid room gives a harmonious impression.

Venetian synagogues also have several special features: all of their exteriors are kept extremely unadorned and they can only be identified by their large arched windows. The synagogue room is placed in the upper floor. In all of them the Torah shrine and the bimah stand opposite one another on the narrow sides: even though this is a sign of Sephardic synagogues it also applies to the Ashkenazi synagogues in Venice. The benches are placed parallel to the long sides in order to leave a large open space in the centre.

Further reading:
"Venice", in: Encyclopaedia Judaica (English), vol. 20, Detroit 2007, pp. 499–504

Riccardo Calimani: The ghetto of Venice, Milan 1988

M. Sarfatti, Gli ebrei nell`Italia fascista, 2002

Anna Vera Sullam, The Venetian Ghetto, Milano 2005

Reuben Roberto Bonfil: Cultural change among the Jews of early modern Italy, Farnham 2010.

Historical note:

After 1500 Jews from the nearby small town of Mestre were allowed to settle once more in the Free Republic of Venice. That said, in 1516 the city council allocated them their own area on the site of a foundry (Italian "Geto"). Hence the name "ghetto".

After they were driven out of the towns in the Holy Roman Empire in the 15th century many German-speaking Jews moved to Northern Italy. This explains why they built their own synagogue in 1525/26. They wanted to maintain their own religious customs and melodies. Within the Jewish community people called these immigrants "tedeschi", i.e. Germans. Synagogues were always meant to be teaching houses: hence the Italian word "scuola", corresponding to the Jewish idiom "Schul" or in eastern Poland, "Schil".

In 1791 the ghetto walls were torn down by French occupying forces, but after 1814 the law forcing Jews to live in their own quarter was not reintroduced. Daniele Manin, a man of Jewish origin, led the revolutionary Republic of Venice in 1848 and 49. Equal rights ruled once again for two years. These rights were declared definitive in 1866 when Venice was united with Italy.

After November 1943 the Fascists deported Italian and German Jews to Birkenau and Auschwitz. In 1945 there were 1,050 Jews living in the city. By 2007 the Jewish community only numbered 500 members. Today the restored synagogues in the ghetto are important tourist attractions. Nearby there is a small Jewish Museum containing valuable ritual objects. It also commemorates the martyrs of the Shoah.

Piatra Neamt, Romania:

Opened: 1766
Architect: unknown
Seating capacity: ca 45

In Eastern Europe there were a huge number of wooden synagogues before 1939, of which very few still exist today. The Baal Shem Tov synagogue in Piatra Neamt is the last remaining wooden synagogue in Romania.

People enter the main rectangular room in the building via a descending staircase. Despite the fact that it is 2 metres below street level the building is 16 metres high. It is possible that the synagogue room was placed in the lower floor because it was forbidden to build synagogues higher than the surrounding buildings in the 18th century. The wooden walls are decorated with colourful flowers.

In the middle of the domed room is a freestanding bimah. Carved gilded lions, griffins, grapes and a huge number of Jewish symbols decorate the elaborately designed Torah shrine made by Schraga Jizchak ben Mosche in 1835.

Legend has it that the founder of Hasidic Judaism, Baal Shem Tov (1698–1760) prayed in a previous stone building located on this spot. The wooden synagogue stands on the foundation walls of this building. Restoration work lasted for eight years and the building was reopened on 14 December 2009.

Further reading:

"Romania", in: Encyclopaedia Judaica (English), Detroit 2007, vol. 17, pp. 375–397

Carol Iancu, Jews in Romania, 1866–1910, 1990

Harry M. Rabinowicz: Hasidism, The movement and its masters, Northvale, NJ 1988

David Berger, The rebbe, the Messiah and the scandal of orthodox indifference, London 2008

Martin Buber, Hasidism and modern man, translated by Maurice Friedman, New York 1966

Simon Dubnow, Geschichte des Chassidismus in zwei Bände, Jüdischer Verlag, Berlin 1931, ND: Frankfurt 1982

Historical note:

Jews began to settle in the area of present-day Romania in ancient times. In the Middle Ages some of them lived in harbour towns on the Black Sea. In the second half of the 15th century many of them immigrated here under Ottoman rule. After pogroms in Poland in 1648/49 the survivors moved south. After 1750 Hasidic Jews joined them from the north. The protest movement was a reaction of simple Jews to the moneyed and intellectual aristocracy in the Jewish communities in Eastern Europe. Their core area was in the south of the kingdom of Poland/Lithuania. (The historic areas were called Podolia, Volhyna and Galicia, now West Ukraine and Northern Romania). The Hasidic groups believed in a hidden "mystic" meaning behind divine teachings. They believed that their rabbis possessed holy names (Hebraic: "Baal Shem") and magic powers.

Martin Buber popularised Hasidic philosophy amongst German-speaking Jews between 1900 and 1938. That said, his folksy translations of Hasidic stories were critically questioned by academics like Gershom Scholem because they were often very free.

Since the 1980s the Lubavitch Hasidim from the USA have had a particularly high profile amongst European Jews because of their highly energetic efforts to convert secular Jews to an ultra-orthodox way of life. Many Jews regard their adoration of Menachem Schneersohn, a dead charismatic personality, in a very critical manner. In addition the creation of parallel religious infrastructures in Western Europe has often led to conflicts within established communities

After 1945 the surviving Jews in Romania emigrated to Israel and the West. In 1956 Romania had 144,000 Jews: in 1992 only 9,000 Jews belonged to a Jewish community.

Worms, Germany:

Opened: 1174/75
Reconstructed and
reopened in 1961
Architect: unknown
Seating capacity:
200 including
the women's synagogue

The original synagogue, built in 1034, was replaced by a new building in 1174/75. It is the earliest example of a mediaeval twin-nave synagogue of its type. The Torah shrine was set in the central axis of the east wall. The bimah stood in the centre of the room between the two supporting columns. It was framed by arcades of pointed arches that no longer exist. In mediaeval Ashkenazi synagogues it was customary for women to gather in their own room for prayers. For this reason a woman's synagogue was built onto the north side of the building in 1212/13. Another annex was built in 1624: this was the so-called Raschi chapel that served as a teaching house.

The synagogue was burned down in 1938 and remained a ruin for many years after. In 1961 it was rebuilt using many parts from the original building. The name of the teaching house is a reminder of the scholar Raschi (1040–1105), who taught in Troyes and Worms. His commentaries on the Hebraic Bible and the Talmud are still considered as standard works.

Further reading:
Fritz Reuter, Jewish Worms. Rashi House and Judengasse, Worms 1992

Joachim Schalk, Der Wormsgau. Sonderheft. Festschrift für Fritz Reuter zum 60. Geburtstag. Worms 1990

Michael Brocke, Der jüdische Friedhof Worms im Mittelalter 10-1519, in: Die SchUM-Gemeinden Speyer – Worms – Mainz: auf dem Weg zum Welterbe Regensburg 2011, pp. 111–154.

Samson Rothschild, Aus Vergangenheit und Gegenwart der Israelitischen Gemeinde Worms, Frankfurt 1926

"Worms", in: Encyclopaedia Judaica (English), Detroit 2007, vol. 8, p. 226f.

Historical note:
Before November 1938 it was the oldest surviving synagogue in Germany: this was the reason it was destroyed by the Nazis. Until 1803 the town was known officially as the Freie Reichsstadt Worms. With the exception of one break Jews lived here continually from the 11th century at the latest until the Nazi persecution began.

That said, the Nazis did nothing to clear up the rubble after the 9th November 1938, and this meant that some of the remnants could be dug out once again. Intensive discussions began about how to reconstruct the building. In 1945 there was no Jewish community in Worms. The Jews who lived there were allocated to the Jewish community in Mainz. Many emigrants opposed the idea of building a synagogue for the (non-Jewish) general public when there was no Jewish community in the town.

The synagogue was reopened in 1961 with an extremely solemn official ceremony. Chancellor Konrad Adenauer donated a curtain for the Torah ark. The site was decorated with Israeli and German flags, although at the time many people in Israel were on principle opposed to rebuilding a Jewish infrastructure in Germany.

On the initiative of the head of the city archives, Fritz Reuter, the site was redeveloped into an ensemble containing the city archives and a permanent exhibition on the history of the Jews in Worms. On special holidays the building was used by Jewish members of the American army in the army base in Ramstein, and it was also infrequently used by individual Jews on private occasions. There is also a ritual immersion bath next to the reconstructed synagogue. The dance house had to be demolished because it had fallen into disrepair. The exterior of the new building is very similar to that of the old: today it also houses the City Museum and archive. A 20 minute walk takes you from here to the "Heiliger Sand" (Holy Sand), the oldest Jewish cemetery in Europe.

New York, USA:

Opened: 1897
Architect: Arnold Brunner
Seating capacity:
unknown

Shearith Israel is the oldest Jewish community in the United States. It was set up in 1654. The community built the current building in the 19th century to cater for the growing number of members. The neo-classicist facade with its tall Corinthian columns and attic finds a corresponding interior in the form of the marble Torah shrine. The overall impression of the space is strengthened by a panelled ceiling.

The prayer room is flooded in light because of the use of bright wood and a high round-arched window. The semi-oval wooden bimah faces west; it thereby corresponds to the Sephardi type of synagogue.

Further reading:
"New York", in: Encyclopaedia Judaica (English) (Detroit 2007), vol. 15, pp. 194–241; Bibliography on the post-1945 period, p. 238 f.

Howard Sachar, A History of the Jews in America, New York 1993.

Historical note:
In the 17th century Jews were allowed to settle under Dutch rule in New Amsterdam, as New York was known at the time. The first Jewish group called itself "Shearith Israel", the "remains of Israel". In 1830 immigrants began arriving in the USA from German-speaking countries. Nonetheless, in comparison with the large urban communities in Europe, the Jewish population in the New York remained relatively small (60,000) until 1880. Between 1880 and 1924 hundreds of thousands of East European Jews moved westwards, many to the USA. The upshot was that by 1928 there were 1,835,000 Jews living in Greater New York; over a quarter of the population. The city now held by far the largest Jewish community in the world.

Mumbai (formerly „Bombay"), India:

Opened: 1886
Architects: Jacob and Albert Sassoon
Seating capacity: unknown

Both the interior and exterior of the synagogue are light blue with white tones. The Torah shrine is fitted into an apse and crowned with colourful glass windows. Since Jerusalem lies to the west of India the shrine is situated near the west wall. The rectangular bimah, surrounded by a wooden balustrade, stands in front of the Torah shrine in the middle of the room, surrounded by benches. It can be entered from the east. The design is strongly reminiscent of classicist synagogue buildings in Europe.

The man who built the synagogue, Jacob Sassoon, gave it the name "Eliyahoo synagogue" in memory of his father, Elias.

Further reading:
Joan Roland, The Jewish Communities of India, New Brunswick NJ 1998.

Historical note:
Jews came to India in the 17th and 18th century to trade in spices from Iraq and Syria. They spoke Arabic and this remained their native tongue. They built their first synagogue in 1796. The Sassoon family was the leading family in Bombay in the 19th century, and was very orientated towards England. Elias (1820–1880) was the oldest son of David Sassoon (1792–1864), who had established a huge merchant bank in the city. Elias, after whom the synagogue was named, lived in China for many years where he was involved in the wool and opium trade. The members of the family lived, and continue to live, in London. European Jews came to Bombay after 1933: in 2007 their number was estimated to be around 2,700.

Budapest, Hungary:

Opened: 1859
Architects:
Ludwig Förster (exterior),
Friedrich Feszl (interior)
Seating capacity:
almost 3,000

The synagogue has various architectural styles, the most dominant of which is Moorish. The form of the building, in the sense of historicism and the symbolic use of styles, was intended to refer to the roots of Judaism in the Near East. Since it is a reform synagogue it has an organ in the West Gallery, which was played by both Franz Liszt and Camille Saint-Saëns. The interior contains a memorial to the Swedish diplomat, Raoul Wallenberg, who saved the lives of many Hungarian Jews during the Nazi period.

Further reading:
"Budapest", in: Encyclopaedia Judaica (English), Detroit 2007, vol. 4, pp. 244–249,

"Budapest": in: Encyclopaedia Judaica (German), vol. 2, specifically pp. 1159–1170.

Historical note:
Until 1939 Budapest was one of the largest Jewish communities in Europe. 267,563 Jews were living there in 1925. A fifth of the city was Jewish. Around 70,000 Jews survived the Shoah. Now the two Jewish communities comprise only 4,000 members between them.

**Amsterdam,
the Netherlands:**

Opened: 1675
Architects: Elias Bouwman
and Daniel Stalpaert
Seating capacity: ca. 1.600

When the Jews were driven out of Spain and Portugal at the end of the 15th century many of them found refuge in the Netherlands. The design is typical of Dutch baroque buildings. The facade is divided by four pilasters. Large arched windows are placed between two rows of small rectangular windows. The interior follows the twin poles scheme of Sephardic synagogues: the bimah is placed towards the West, opposite the Torah shrine at the East wall. Hence there is plenty of room for the benches in the centre, which are lined parallel to the longitudinal side of the prayer room. Portuguese synagogues influenced other synagogue buildings, including those in Livorno, London (the Bevis Marks synagogue), the Hague and New York (Central Park West). The oldest active Jewish library, the Etz Hayim library, is situated in the synagogue complex.

Further reading:
"Amsterdam", in: Encyclopaedia Judaica (German), vol. 2, pp. 716–734: and Encyclopaedia Judaica (English), Detroit 2007, vol. 2, pp. 106–120.

Historical note:
80,000 Jews lived in Amsterdam until 1941. 90% of Dutch Jews were murdered. In 2000 the number of Jewish residents in Amsterdam was reckoned to be around 20,000, but only 4,500 of these are members of Orthodox and liberal communities. 450 of them can be attributed to the old "Portuguese" community. Their number rose following immigration from Israel and Morocco. In 1984 the Jewish Historical Museum was opened: it is had a positive influence on the cultural development of Jews in Amsterdam. http://www.jhm.nl/english.aspx

Amongst others, the Jewish Historical Museum consists of an Ashkenazi Synagogue, and adjacent buildings. It co-manages the organisation of guided tours and visits to the Portuguese Synagogue.

Jerusalem, Israel:

Opened: 2000
Architect: Isaac Blatt
Seating capacity: 6.000

The Great Synagogue belonging to the Belz Hasidics, an ultra-orthodox community, is the largest synagogue in Jerusalem. The building is a replica of the synagogue in Belz (Ukraine), built by Rebbe Shalom Rokeach (1799–1835) in 1843. Its exterior is strongly reminiscent of the, then contemporary, ideas of the shape of the ancient temple in Jerusalem.

Inside the giant space within the rectangular building is a richly decorated Torah shrine, twelve metres high and weighing eighteen tonnes. It can hold 70 Torah scrolls. Each of the nine candelabras (5.5 metres tall × 3.4 metres wide), is made of more than 200,000 pieces of Czech crystal. There are three galleries, from which the women and children can follow the services. The building also contains libraries, halls for festivities, and smaller prayer rooms that are used on weekdays. Several stories contain living rooms. Dormitory-style bedrooms are available to Belz Hasidics who come to study religion in Israel.

Further reading:
"Belz", in: Encyclopaedia Judaica (English), Detroit 2007, vol. 3, p. 308 f.

Historical note:
In 1944 Aaron Rokeach, a descendant of the Belz Rebbe, succeeded in fleeing to Palestine. Other Hasidic Jews from Belz had emigrated to Brooklyn in the 1920s and 30s. In Israel the Belz Hasidim support the orthodox party, Agudat Israel.

Further general literature on synagogues:

Eschwege, Helmut: Die Synagoge in der deutschen Geschichte. Eine Dokumentation, Dresden 1988

Hammer-Schenk, Harold: Synagogen in Deutschland. Geschichte einer Baugattung im 19. und 20. Jahrhundert. 2 vols., Hamburg 1981

Krinsky, Carol Herselle: Synagogues of Europe: architecture, history, meaning, New York 1985

On the liturgy:

Elbogen, Ismar: Jewish Liturgy. A comprehensive history, transl. by Raymond Scheindlin, Philadelphia 1993

Böckler, Annette: Jüdischer Gottesdienst. Wesen und Struktur, Berlin 2002

German translations of Jewish liturgy:

Orthodox: Siddur Schma Kolenu, Zürich/Basel 1991–2007 (Albert Richter, Josef Scheuer), the liturgy on Jewish holidays was also translated.

Liberal: Seder ha-Tefillot. Das jüdische Gebetbuch, ed. by Rabbis Jonathan Magonet and Walter Homolka, Gütersloh 1997, vol. I (Schabbat, Wochentage und Pilgerfeste) und II (Hohe Feiertage)

For a synagogue choir in the old German-Jewish tradition, see the "Israelitische Cultusgemeinde Zürich" (ICZ): Internet: www.synagogenchor.ch

A traditional and a liberal synagogue

Wooden model of the Essen synagogue at Steeler Tor, built 1911–1913, opened in 1913, interior destroyed in 1938. Scale 1:50. Made by students at the Technical University in Braunschweig in 2002 (Bet Tfila research department at the Technical University Braunschweig, Uwe Knufinke), http://www.bet-tfila.org/

Wooden model of the synagogue in Halberstadt, Bakenstraße, opened in 1712, destroyed in 1938/39. Scale 1:50. Made by Dipl.-Ing. Andrea Jensen, Braunschweig, 2010. (With the kind support of the Bet Tfila research department at the Technical University Braunschweig, Uwe Knufinke), http://www.bet-tfila.org/

Glass case, Colin Steiner, glass rectangle, 50 × 130 × 50 × 130 cm

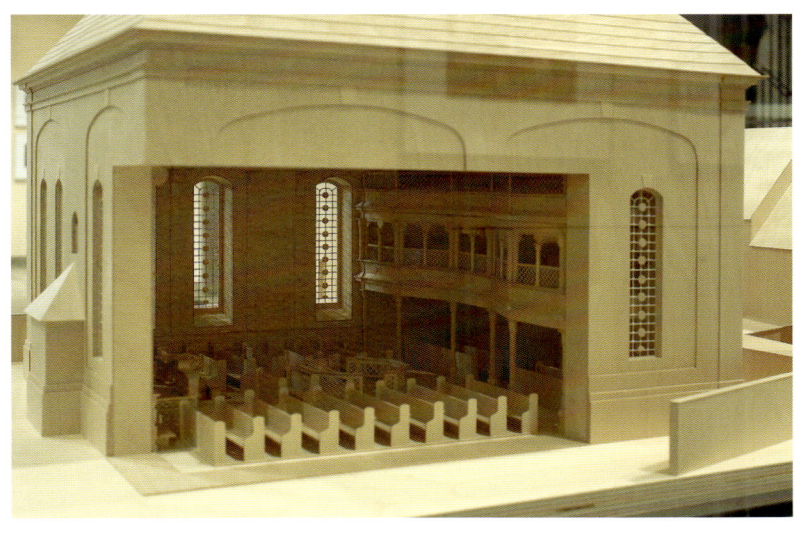

A wooden model of the Essen synagogue with historical furnishing, back garden with Sukkah and entrance courtyard

A wooden model of the baroque synagogue in Halberstadt with its central lectern and strongly screened-off women's gallery

Reconstructed pillars in the interior with the reprographies from the Festschrift edited by Edmund Körner (1914)

The supporting walls beneath the former women's gallery

Here you can see magnified photos of the interior of the Essen synagogue as it was before 1938; uniform size 87 x 115.5 cm. Some of them are from the 1914 Festschrift (commemorative publication): "Neue Synagoge Essen Ruhr mit Text von Richard Klapheck", 13. Sonderheft der Architektur des XX. Jahrhunderts, published by Ernst Wasmuth A.G. Berlin W 8 (1914).

Descriptions can be found, starting from the entrance, and running clockwise from the north

North side

The first supporting wall looking left from the entrance.
West side: A view of the Torah ark and organ. Vertical format. In Festschrift Körner p. 78: "The Holy of Holies"

Introduction: What is a Synagogue?

East side: Cupola and organ with round ornaments. Horizontal format. In Festschrift Körner p.75: "Looking towards the cupola"

Sceond supporting wall.
West side: Front of the women's gallery with Hebrew mosaic. Horizontal format, not in Festschrift.

East side: Rear of the women's gallery. Vertical format. In Festschrift Körner p.72: "View of the interior"

South side

The first supporting wall seen from the Torah ark.
East side: View of the Torah ark and Menorah. Horizontal format. (In Festschrift Körner p. 64: "The view on entering the very interior of the temple".

West side: A large window, theme: "Shabbat" with two Menoras (seven-branched candlesticks), Kinnor (King David Harp). Vertical format, not in Festschrift, but cf. Architektur – Kultur – Religion. Ein Spaziergang durch die Alte Synagoge, Essen 2010, p. 38 f. (co-authors incl. Matthias Kohn)

Second supporting wall.
East side: View from the women's gallery onto the Torah ark with organ and candlesticks. Horizontal format, not in Festschrift,

West side: View from below of the Torah shrine and window with two candlesticks, paintings in the panels. Vertical format. In Festschrift Körner p. 68: "From within"

Historic glass panels. These pictures can now be found in the Ruhr Museum at "Zeche Zollverein" (section on photos of Essen). In 1939 they were sold to the city by Heinrich Lehmkühler. Some photographs may be by his master Heinrich Fleischhauer (information from Horst Bühne, Stiftung Ruhr Museum, photo archives 28th April 2016)

A memorial corner: four commemorative books

Commemorative books (2005), written between 1985 and 2005 as part of a project with school students and adults from Essen, including descendants. Four volumes, three of which have biographies (94, 138 and 135 pages). The other volume contains an alphabetical index of names (pp. 5–94, around 2,300 biographies, some of families), 123 pages.
All four volumes: 23,5 × 22 cm, white laminated

The books were designed like Jewish "Yizkor" books ("Yizkor", Hebrew for "May (God) remember"). Yizkor is recited in the synagogue four times a year in remembrance of relatives that have passed on (Memorial service for the souls of the Dead, Hebrew "Hazkarat Neschamot"): The books are intended to be a part of this tradition. Around 1,700 of the 4,500 Jews who lived in Essen in 1925 had emigrated by 1939. Presumably around 2,500 of those who remained were murdered.

The empty Torah Ark

In 1960 the Jugendstil Torah ark was taken down to make room for the new House of Industrial Design. Körner's gold mosaic was also removed and disappeared. The ark was only reconstructed – on the basis of old photos – in 1986 when a new concept for the house was decided on. Translated into English the Hebraic inscription reads: "Know before whom you stand." The lion stands for the tribe of Judah: as a royal animal it demands respect for the sacred teachings. A conscious decision was made not to commission new Torah scrolls. The empty ark is intended to show visitors that the Old Synagogue is no longer used for religious purposes.

The stage-like design is typical of 19th-century synagogues. A new feature of these "modern" synagogues was that the Torah scrolls were not read out to the community from the centre of the building. The synagogue built in 1810 in Seesen (the Harz region), was designed according to this new pattern and set the style for synagogues in German-speaking regions. Orthodox synagogues were the exception. Because they wanted to keep their own specific profile they kept to the traditional spatial structure with the lectern in the middle. After 1945 the majority of new synagogues in German were built according to the traditional pattern.

A Jewish community should have at least three perfectly written ("kosher") Torah scrolls.

The Torah ark. It was reconstructed in 1986 from photographs.

Old Synagogue Essen – House of Jewish Culture

Sources of Jewish Traditions

Inscription:

Maintaining traditions is a basic element of every culture. Jewish traditions cover a 5,000 year history. What sources do they draw on?

The exhibition section entitled Sources of Jewish Traditions provides insights into four large thematic areas:

1. Jewish history (including Jewish personalities) as a defining source of a Jewish sense of identity

2. Traditional texts and objects used in religious and cultural practice

3. The Jewish calendar is a common framework for Jews all over the world, also in respect of their connection to the land of Israel

4. The central rites in the cycle of life, like birth, maturity, marriage and death

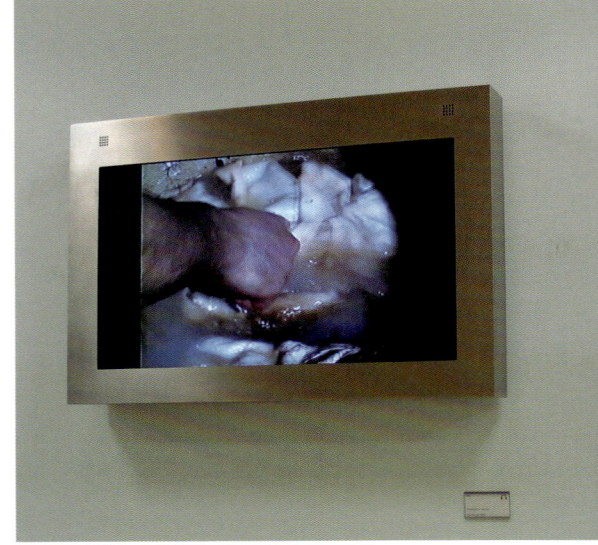

This section explains how Torah scrolls, megillas (scrolls of the Book of Esther etc.) and mezuzot (parchments left in a small case by the door post of a house) are made. An excerpt on Jewish orthodoxy from an American documentary film shows the making of a Torah scroll.

The relationship between the Jewish and Christian calendars is explained by a large installation with two metal wheels on one of the side walls.

To the left of this, on the wall, a touch screen enables visitors to move backwards and forwards in time between the Jewish and Christian calendar. Made by Israel Hersch, 2009. www.kalnach.net

On the west side of the room there is an original old broadsheet (Hungary 1905, "Ref: Lazar Rapaport, Bartfeld (Hungary)", printed in Kolomea/Galicia (then Austro/Hungary). For 50 years it was used to reckon on what Christian date a Jewish date falls.

The direction of prayer towards Jerusalem was indicated in traditional Jewish houses. Hence in Europe it was always East (Hebrew: "Mizrah"). In

An enlarged mizrah (a sign marking the direction of prayer), based on a silhouette cut out by Chaim Katz Silbiger, Poland 1891, made by Eva Sand, 2010

"Metal silhouettes", made by Colin Steiner, Berlin, 2011

Monitor: Film on the making of a Torah scroll (English), "Let's write a Torah", produced by Sholom Ber Goldstein (USA) no year given (DVD)

Jewish and Christian calendars: two wheels installation

Video on how to write a Torah scroll, phylacteries and texts for doorposts, "mezuzot"

The rectangular glass cases in the middle of the room:

Dressed Torah with sign (replica)

Oriental Torah scroll made of goat's leather, with an ornamental feature (finial), probably from North Africa (fragment), found in an attic in France.
At the bottom of the case: quills and an inkpot

    A Torah scroll has vowel signs to tell you how to pronounce the text. The person speaking the prayer has to know these passages by heart or learn them on Friday before reciting them on Shabbat (Saturday). During the service a member of the board uses the printed text to follow the reading and, where necessary, interrupts to correct the pronunciation.

Glass case in the area
Sources of Jewish Traditions: Torah scroll

Glass cases in area *Sources of Jewish Traditions:*
necessary things to pray (shawl, prayer books with translations, kippot, phylacteries), Torah scroll, Hanukkiah/Menorah, Torah scroll for children, feathers and ink, decorated Torah scroll with shield ("tass") and Yad

Sources of Jewish Traditions

Old Synagogue Essen – House of Jewish Culture 149

150 *Sources of Jewish Traditions*

The rectangular glass cases (Fortsetzung):

Torah equipment

Prayer accessories

Hanukkiah/Menorah

Circumcision: an original circumcision book from the Netherlands.

Bar-/Bat-Mitzvah: In Israel thirteen-years olds from a religious milieu often receive a book explaining readings from the Torah. Only a few Jewish young people are capable of reading an excerpt from the Torah aloud in the traditional "trop" (or melody). As a rule they only speak the blessing before and after the reading of the Torah excerpt.

Wedding contract: marriages are legally sealed in a ketubba, a special type of Jewish prenuptial agreement written according to a standard formula.

Burials: The Jewish community puts an eternal grave at the disposal of its members. According to traditional precepts the corpse is washed and dressed. In traditional families, the bride gives her husband burial robes ("sargenes") when they marry. Dead souls are remembered in a special ceremony four times a year.

Glass cases showing the stations of life: first row: circumcision, Bar-/Bat Mitzvah, second row: marriage, burial customs

Mohel-book from the Netherlands (register of circumcisions), 18th century

152   *Sources of Jewish Traditions*

Southern Wall: installation

Along the side wall facing south there is an installation with English translations. This gives a comprehensive chronology of Jewish history from the time of Abraham to 2008. There are also references to the history of anti-Judaism and the Zionist movement.

A large glass case shows the names and portraits of Jewish personalities from ancient times to 2007

Glass panel with the names of 360 Jewish personalities

Timeline of Jewish history from Abraham to 2008

There are a total of 18 × 20 personalities (i.e. 360 names), all with key life dates, where known. Where possible, there is also a picture. They include men and women, scholars and secular Jews, those who have followed a career in politics; and others who made a name for themselves in Jewish intellectual history. A touch screen will provide more detailed biographical information.

Old Synagogue Essen – House of Jewish Culture

Former Women's Gallery: *Jewish Holidays*

Inscription:

Traditional holidays are important anchor points in the Jewish calendar. Many of them are connected with agricultural aspects in Israel. They thereby express a particular bond with the Land of Israel.

Jewish holidays recall significant dates in the history of their community and uphold the memory of collective experiences and identities. In the Old Synagogue the high significance of Jewish holidays was once marked by six original stained-glass windows above the women's gallery, each dedicated to a major holiday. These stained-glass windows are now lost and can no longer be reconstructed. But Jewish holidays are once more thematised in the women's gallery. The section of the exhibition entitled *Jewish Holidays* is contained in six glass cases featuring eight selected holidays:
– Shabbat
– Purim
– Passover and Shavuot
– Rosh ha-Shanah and Yom Kippur
– Sukkoth
– Hanukkah

Outline overview of the arrangement. Clockwise from North to South:

Shabbat

Shabbat, the seventh day of the week, is a day of rest to remind believers that God rested on the seventh day of Creation. (2. Book of Moses 20, 8–10). At the same time it recalls their liberation from slavery in Egypt (5. Book of Moses 5, 15). It begins on Friday evening before dusk and ends on Saturday evening after nightfall as soon as three stars can be clearly seen.

In ancient times slaves, non-Jews and working animals also had a right to a day of rest. The decisive factor here is the definition of the word "work". There are discussions and definitions in the Mishnah and Talmud as to what activities constitute "work".

For this reason Shabbat is not a day of rest in the sense of doing nothing at all, but much more in the sense of pausing, ceasing everyday activities and reflecting on essentials. Prohibitions take second place behind having a pleasant day in clear contrast to a working day. Shabbat is a day of joy. This is in utterly different from the unfriendly characterisation attributed to it by old Christian theologians.

Start of Shabbat

In traditional families, the wife lights two Shabbat candles and speaks a blessing over the light shortly before the start of Shabbat on Friday evening.

In synagogue services on Friday evening Shabbat is solemnly welcomed like a bride or a queen.

After returning home from the synagogue and a brief ceremony the family begins Shabbat. A blessing is spoken over the wine in the Kiddush cup, which is then passed around the table. Then a blessing is spoken over two loaves of braided bread ("berkhes" or "challah") on the table. The loaves symbolise the manna that fell from heaven whilst the Israelis were wandering in the desert. At the time, on the sixth day – i.e. Friday – there was twice the amount of manna so that it did not have to be gathered on Shabbat.

Many prayers are spoken at the Shabbat morning service in the synagogue, and there are two readings from the Hebrew Bible: the weekly reading of a section from the Torah and a suitable excerpt from one of the books of the Prophets ("Haftara"). The service, which is given in Hebrew, lasts around two and a half hours as a rule, not including the "talk on the Torah", (D'var Torah).

End of Shabbat: the Havdalah ("separation")

On Saturday evening the celebrants stand in front of a braided candle (it has two wicks) to bless the wine. After the spices in the besamim container have been blessed they are passed around to spread the sweet-smelling Shabbat perfumes into the profane weekday world. Blessing the light and speaking the blessing marks the end of Shabbat, after which the candle is extinguished by pouring a little wine over it.

Exhibits:
Candleholder: Inv. no. 76
Four Kiddush cups: Inv. nos. 69–71, 75
Breadcutting set: Inv. no. 79
Havdalah sets, porcelain, three-part, no. 87, four-part: Inv. nos. 65, 66, 68
Besamim containers (Spice containers): Inv. nos. 72–74.
Light switch cover: Inv. no. 77
Two Shabbat and Havdalah travelling sets: Inv. nos. 78, 287
Two braided Havdalah candles: Inv. no. 287
Challa/Berkhes made from salt dough: Inv. no. 286

Glass case: Purim

Clothes for the Queen Ester and rattles for making a noise when reciting the name of the evil person Haman

Jewish Holidays

Purim

The Purim holiday commemorates the saving of the Jewish community in Persia from Haman, the royal vizier to King Ahasuerus/Achashverosh (presumed to be Artaxerxes I of Persia). The events, which are related in the Book of Esther, are supposed to have taken place around 450 BCE. The name Purim is derived from the word "pur" (Engl. lot), for Haman drew lots to pick the date on which all the Jews in Persia were to be murdered. Only thanks to the intervention of the King's wife, a Jewess named Esther, could the plans be foiled at the last moment.

The Purim story can be interpreted as symbolising the situation of Jews in the many lands of the Diaspora, where their lives often depend(ed) on the mood of the ruler or the people. Thanks to the surprising twist in the story, Purim is a festival of joy emphasising solidarity and friendship.

In synagogues and religious schools the Book of Esther is read out from a scroll. Children traditionally make a noise to blot out Haman's name whenever it is mentioned: for example they shake rattles.

On the holiday it is usual to present gifts to the needy. Food and drink is given to friends and relatives. Children exchange gifts of sweets packed in bags decorated with motifs from the Purim story.

A further custom says that you should eat, drink alcohol and be happy. "Hamantaschen" – sweet triangular pastries filled with poppy seed, fruit and nuts – are a typical Purim dish. Putting on plays, comic "Purimspiele", and dressing up are favourite activities amongst children. In the old days they used to dress up as Esther and her uncle Mordechai, the heroes of the book of Esther. Nowadays all types of dressing-up and carnival-type processions through the streets are customary. There is a huge amount of colourfully illustrated editions of the Book of Esther, some of which contain details on customs surrounding the Purim festivities. Small scrolls are also printed for children.

Exhibits:
Four Purim rattles (one with Inv. no. 276, the others without Inv. no.)
Paper carrier bag: Inv. no. 276
Printed Esther scroll: Inv. no. 275
Instruction for wine blessings on Shabbat and holidays (including Purim), Israel 1999: without Inv. no.
Purim dress, pink: without Inv. no.

Passover and Shavuot

Passover and Shavuot are two of the three ancient pilgrimage festivals at the Temple in Jerusalem where the first fruits of the harvest were brought.
(3. Moses 23,10).

Passover is an agricultural festival (Hebrew: "Hag ha'aviv"), held in spring to mark the first fruits of the barley in the land of Israel. Historically and theologically it is regarded as the Feast of Liberation from Slavery. The liberation from Egypt is traditionally regarded as a seminal myth by the People of Israel.

The word Passover comes from the Hebrew "passah", to pass through or pass over, a reference to the Tenth Plague, the slaying of the firstborn of Egypt, when the angel of God passed by the houses of the Jews, i.e. deliberately overlooked them.

Mezuzas (doorposts) serve to recall this event. On many Jewish houses and flats and on almost every doorway in these dwellings people hang a long thin casing on the right-hand doorpost. Inside is a parchment containing verses from the Fifth Book of Moses 6, 4–9 and 11, 13–21, written by hand in Hebrew.

Passover is celebrated over seven days in Israel, and eight days in the Jewish Diaspora. It begins with the Seder evening that is mostly celebrated in families, with friends and, more recently, frequently in Jewish communities. Everyone reads the Passover Haggadah, a collection of texts from the Jewish Bible, other traditional writings, blessings and songs. The Hebrew word "seder" means "order" since the events in the festivity have a distinct order. The book explains the origins of the festival and instructions on the running order of the Seder evening.

Its texts are read out loud in turn – each according to family traditions and partly in the national language. The songs are sung together.

The food made especially for Passover has a particular significance. One example is matzo, a piece of flat unleavened bread, for which there are special plates and bags. It is customary to place three matzos in a bag, each of which is marked with the name Cohen, Levi or Israel. The matzo in the middle, also known as "Afikoman", is hidden so that the children have to look for it. Other symbolic dishes for this meal are placed on a special plate known as the Seder Plate.

In traditional families the crockery is changed for these days in order to avoid eating leavened food. The kitchen must also have been thoroughly cleaned and anything leavened removed.

Shavuot

The Feast of Weeks begins seven times seven days after Passover. This calculation (reckoned from Easter) has been taken over into the Christian calendar as Whitsun.

Historically Shavuot is a harvest festival since this marks the start of the wheat harvest in the Land of Israel. The first fruits of the wheat harvest were brought to the Temple in Jerusalem. Historically and theologically the festival recalls God's gift of the Torah to the people of Israel on Mount Sinai as a sign of

Glass case for the Passover and Shavuot holidays

A Passover plate from the year 1814, replica of Israel Museum, Jerusalem

the bond between them. According to the Bible God gave Moses two stone tablets on which the Ten Commandments were engraved. Later traditions speak of the complete Torah.

The relevant portion of the Torah is read aloud in the synagogue (2. Moses, 19–20). Everyone stands for the reading of the Ten Commandments as the people of Israel once did on Mount Sinai. Typical Shavuot motifs, like Moses holding the tablets with the Ten Commandments, can be found on Torah breast plates, as well as on decorated plates. The custom of decorating the synagogue for Shavuot with flowers and green plants recalls the bringing of the first fruits of the wheat harvest to the Temple in Jerusalem. Seven types of plants characterize the Land of Israel: barley, wheat, grapes, figs, pomegranates, olives and dates. Paper-cuts featuring plant and animal motifs are also popular.

Exhibits:
Seder plates
Pewter plate
Porcelain plate
Haggadot, facsimile, new print
The seven types of plant (sheva minim)

A Shavuot plate: the holiday is related to the revelation of the Torah on Mount Sinai. This is why Moses is holding the stone tablets with the Ten Commandments. Replica of one in the Israel Museum, Jerusalem

Jewish Holidays

Glass case for Rosh ha-Shanah and Yom Kippur

Different types of Shofarot and new prayer book ("Mahzor") for Yom Kippur with German translation ("Schma Kolenu", Zurich 2007)

Rosh ha-Shanah and Yom Kippur

Along with Yom Kippur (the Day of Atonement), Rosh ha-shanah (New Year) is one of the major Jewish religious holidays. There are ten days between the two (the ten days of atonement and contemplation, "Asseret Jemei ha-Teshuva"), dedicated to reflection and changing one's ways. In orthodox synagogues the penitential prayer ("Selichot") is recited at dawn. In the previous Jewish month, Elul, people visit the graves of the forefathers.

Rosh ha-Shanah is celebrated over two days when pieces of apple dipped in honey are traditionally eaten. In doing so people wish each other a "good and sweet (New) Year" ("le-shana tova u-metuka").

According to tradition two books are opened at the coming of the New Year – one for the righteous, the other for the evil. All Jews are then judged for their deeds in the previous year and their names are written in one of the books. A change of habits, a prayer and an act of charity can influence the judgement sealed on Yom Kippur.

During the High Holy Days the shofar, a hollowed-out ram's horn, is sounded on several occasions.

Old Synagogue Essen – House of Jewish Culture   161

Yom Kippur, the day of atonement, was first described in the Torah (3rd book of Moses, 16). On this day the High Priest brought sacrifices to purify the Jerusalem Temple and entered the Holy of Holies where he spoke the penitential prayers. This custom has not been carried out since the destruction of the Temple.

Yom Kippur is a day of rest and fasting. Here the Torah only gives a precept "and thou shalt fast". Traditionally Jewish persons over the age of 13 fast "from evening to evening", i.e. they eat and drink nothing. Before fasting begins it is customary to have an early evening meal before sunset. This custom is also observed by many secular Jews, since many of them visit the synagogue during the holy days, something they otherwise very rarely do. (The so-called "Three Days of Jewishness").

The shofar, a hollowed-out ram's horn, recalls Isaac's bond with Abraham (1st book of Moses 22). Yemenite shofar horns are made from the longer, twisted horn of an antelope.

Four different notes are sounded in a prescribed order: Teki'a (a long even tone), Shwarim (three short tones), Tru'a (nine to twelve very short tones) and Teki'a gedolah (a very long even tone). As a rule this honorary office is carried out by specially trained persons. In traditional communities the shofar is not sounded on Shabbat, the day of rest, because this would be regarded as work.

Exhibits:
Tallit and Kippah.
The tallit (prayer shawl) is normally only worn for morning prayers during readings from the Torah, except at Yom Kippur when it is worn in the synagogue on the night before. Pious men wear a white garment in the synagogue at Yom Kippur. This is the so-called "kittel" or "sargenes".
Tallit/prayer shawl. Inv. no. 61
Kippah
Ashkenazi shofar. Inv. no. 60
Ashkenazi shofar. No inventory number.
Yemenite shofar. Inv. no. 283
Rosh ha-Shanah plate for apples and honey. Inv. no. 46
Eight-piece plush set for Rosh ha-Shanah. Inv. no. 281: Round loaf as a symbol for the cycles on the year, candle holder, a jar of honey with an apple and a worm. Traditionally people wish each other a "good and sweet New Year".
Prayer book for Yom Kippur with a German translation, 1890: W.(olf) Heidenheim, Prayers for the Atonement evening, 1890, opened on the page of the prayer, "Our Father, our King". Alternative: Mahzor "Schma Kolenu", Zurich 2011: the first German post-war translation of the Holy Day liturgy by Rabbi Josef Scheuer and Albert Richter.
Prayer book for Rosh ha-Shanah and Yom Kippur for young people: Machsor le-ze'irim le-Rosh ha-Shanah u-le-jom hakippurim Israel 1986

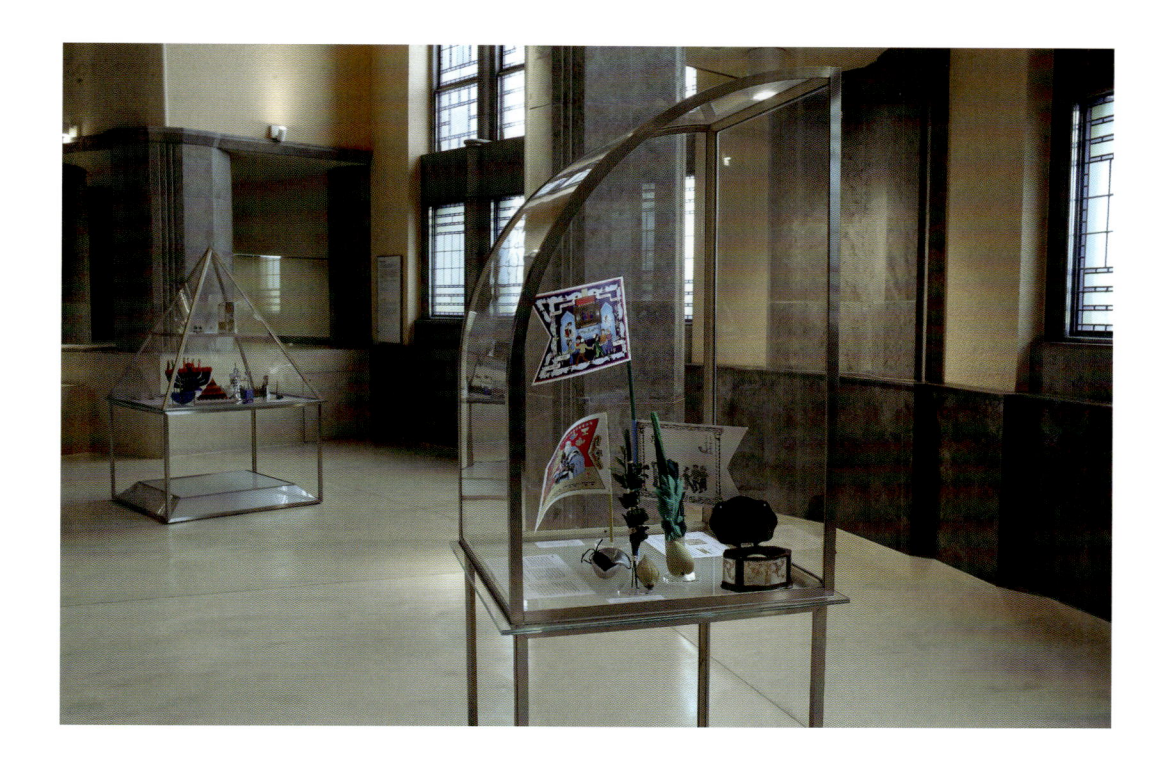

Sukkoth/Simchat Torah

Sukkoth, the Feast of Tabernacles, is first mentioned in the Tora. It is one of the three ancient pilgrimage days at the Jerusalem temple. It takes place in autumn, in the time between the fruit and olive harvests, (or the grape harvest in Israel). Seen from an agricultural point of view it is therefore a harvest thanksgiving festival. The celebrations last for eight days.

The historical and theological aspects are mentioned in the Tora (3rd book of Moses 23, 39–43). Sukkas (huts of temporary construction with a roof covering of branches) recall the time when the People of Israel wandered through the desert after leaving Egypt. This is why everyone is expected to live in temporary huts for the duration of the festival. In Central Europe it is customary to take the three daily meals in a Sukkah. If the weather allows, pious men even sleep in the Sukkah. The roof on the hut is covered with branches to enable people to see the sky. The huts can be erected in courtyards, gardens, on flat roofs or on balconies. Besides private huts, Jewish communities frequently build large huts in the synagogue courtyard, where many members of the community can celebrate together. The interior of the huts are decorated with fruit, lanterns, and garlands and pictures made by children. On the final days of the festival the children are allowed to "plunder" the huts and eat the fruit.

Glass case for Sukkoth, the Feast of Tabernacles: a "lulav" bouquet, with Citrus fruit ("Etrog"), paper flags for children for Simchat Torah

A lulav is an integral part of the Feast of Tabernacles. It consists of a palm frond, three a twig of myrtle and one of willow rods, all of which are bound together. The lulav symbolises the different types of vegetation in the Land of Israel. It is taken to the synagogue to be blessed on the first day of Sukkoth. An "etrog" (citrus fruit) is needed for the necessary blessings.

Sukkoth closes with another holiday, Simchat Torah, the Joy of the Torah. This day marks the end of the annual cycle of Torah readings in the synagogue. The opening section of the 1st Book of Moses is read immediately after reading the last section of the 5th Book of Moses. It is a great honour to be called on to read the first section as the so-called "hatan Torah" (bridegroom of the Torah). Persons who have given exceptional service to the community are generally honoured here. All the Torah scrolls are taken from the Torah ark and taken around the lectern seven times. Children also take part in the procession: instead of carrying the Torah scrolls they take articles like flags with pictures of the Torah.

Exhibits:
Two Lulav bundles. Inv. non. 319, 320.
A celebration bundle made of plush. Inv. no. 282
Flags for Simchat Torah. Inv. no. 43 and no inventory number.
Two etrog tins. No inventory number.
Two etrog forms of ceramics (citrus fruit). No inventory number.

Lulav (symbolic plants for the Feast of Tabernacles) and containers for Etrog

Jewish Holidays

Hanukkah

The Hanukkah (dedication) feast is also known as the Festival of Lights. Its origins are described in the 1st Book of the Maccabees, when Judas Maccabeus led the successful revolt in the Land of Israel against the ruling Seleucid Empire and conquered Jerusalem in 165 BCE. He purified and rededicated the temple, removed the heathen altar and had burnt offerings brought to the new altar. He required a pure ritual oil to light the candelabras. According to one legend, there was only a single can of oil left, whose contents were sufficient for just one day. Thanks to a miracle the contents enabled the candles to stay lit for eight days until new oil became available.

This is why Hanukkah is celebrated for eight days. The Hanukkah Menorah (Hanukkiah) has eight branches and an additional branch for the shamash (ser-

The Hanukkah glass case

Different Hanukkah candlesticks and oil lamps
(Moroccan, late medieval Ashkenasi, post modern, 1950's style etc.)

vant) candle, that is used to light the other candles. The Menorah should stand in front of the house door, or at least be visible in the window.

There are a number of different traditional ways of lighting the Menorah. Some people only light the "servant" candle and one other candle on the first evening, followed by an additional candle on every evening after that. Others light all the candles on the first evening and extinguish one candle on every successive evening.

Hanukkah is a popular family holiday, during which special songs are sung. Dishes baked with oil (as a reminder of the eight-day miracle of the oil) is eaten. These include latkes (potato pancakes) and sufganiyot (jelly doughnuts). Children play with a dreidel (spinning top).

Exhibits:
Eight Hanukkah candelabra. Inv. numbers 8–16, 18, 285.
Hanukkah calendar
Baking shapes
Five dreidel (spinning tops). Inv. numbers 19–23.

Former Organ Gallery: *History of the Building*

Inscription:

The long domed building has suffered a turbulent history since it was opened as a synagogue on the 25th September 1913. It ranges from the final years of the Wilhelmine Empire through the Weimar Republic and the so-called Third Reich of the Nazis, up to and including the Federal Republic of Germany.

The building was only used as a synagogue and centre of local Jewish life during the first twenty-five years of its existence until 1938. This was followed by numerous destructions and architectural changes, all of which can be interpreted as the dealings of the majority non-Jewish society with Jewish culture and the Jewish cultural monument in Essen.

The exhibition area entitled History of the Building uses old photos and original exhibits to tell of the changes made to the old synagogue building. A station with screens is available for anyone wishing to go deeper into the subject.

Along the wall you can find documents and objects from the first outline design to the documents outlining the design of the new permanent exhibition that opened in July 2010. A small bust of Edmund Körner stands in the North-East corner.

A beamer depicts the history of the house in the circles on the ceiling (they used to be painted). The best way to look at these is by reclining on one of the wooden deckchairs.

The glass cases along the wall show exhibits on the history of the building. The interactive touch screens in front of the couches offer further texts, drawings and illustrations.

The former organ gallery with the touch screens in the *History of the Building* section

Alte Synagoge Essen – Haus Jüdischer Kultur

Here there is an opportunity to look at further images and read original sources

The exhibits above and in the glass cases along the wall:
Design scheme 1910
Newspaper article on the architecture competition 1908
Three beer bottles from the building period (found during renovations in 2008)
Bust of Edmund Körner (1874–1940)
Document marking the laying of the foundation stone, 1911 (Facsimile of a duplicate from the city archives)
Two original balusters (architectural decoration) from the balcony of the Rabbi's house, ca 1912/13
Booklet with the Liturgy for the Opening Ceremony on 25.9.1913
Pamphlet: Pageant "Salomon" by Rabbi Emil Bernhard Cohn, presented on the 25.9.1913 in the Saalbau
13th special edition of Architektur des 20. Jahrhunderts on the Essen Synagogue, ed. Edmund Körner/Richard Klapheck, 1914
Pieces of mosaic and glass shards, collected in 1938 by Doris Moses, later married name Lissauer, presented as a gift in 1988 (see module in the Lehrhaus Judentum für Kinder)
Fragments of the Torah scrolls and prayer books, picked up on the 10.11.1938 and handed over to the Old Synagogue in the 1980s
Sign: "Forum" (Bildender Künstler). Artists had rooms in the Old Synagogue between 1961 and 2003
Information board on the building, 1980
Plaque sarcophagus, 1981
Award: European Museum of the Year, 1991
Commendation from the society "Germany. Land of Ideas" 2012
Publications of the Old Synagogue between 1980 and 2008

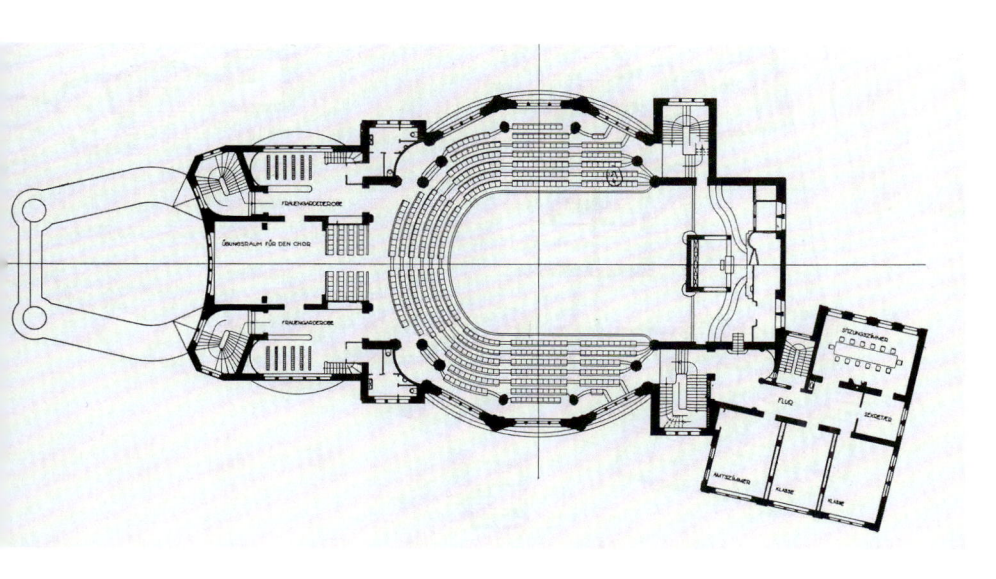

Edmund Körner's plans showing the intended usage of the rooms

Bronze bust of the architect Edmund Körner, from the family estate

Texts, illustrations and photos in the Infostation (1913–2010):
1913–1938
Plan of the synagogue predecessor in the Weberstraße (city archives)
Architectural drawing, 1910. Layout plan of the site
Allgemeine Zeitung des Judentums, 1.3.1908
Photo: building site, 1910 ("Flashoff'sche Villa")
Competition outlines: from the General-Anzeiger für Essen und Umgegend, 4.7.1908
The designs for the new synagogue in Essen: from the Anzeiger für Essen und Umgegend, 6.7.1908
Photo Edmund Körner
Clear Lines for New Buildings. 90 years since the architect Edmund Körner came to Essen: in the Westdeutsche Allgemeine Zeitung (WAZ), 18.12.1998
Edmund Körner. Plan, model and drawing
Ground floor layout, 1910, sheet 3
Plan for the reinforced concrete work, 1912
Group photo of builders, 11.7.1911
Photo of the opening ceremony, 1913
View of the scaffolding form the Rabbi's house, ca 1912
Document marking the laying of the foundation stone, 11.7.1911
Photos of the building site, 1912/13
Letter from Edmund Körner to the city building inspectors, April 1913
Rabbi Dr. Samuel, a review of the history of the building of the synagogue from 1904 until its opening in 1913
Photo: The newly completed synagogue, 1913
Roll of honour for donors to the synagogue, 1913

After 1947/48 survivors were given rooms in the former extension for the rabbi and the board

Liturgy for the opening ceremony (Essen 1913)
Booklet on the pageant "Salomo" (Essen 1913)
Article from the Essener Volkszeitung, 27.9.1913
Report on the opening in the Allgemeine Zeitung des Judentums, 1.10.1913
Rabbi Emil Cohn, The New Synagogue in Essen: from the Allgemeine Zeitung des Judentums, 1913
Richard Klapheck, The New Synagogue in Essen: in Verein für Denkmalpflege und Heimatschutz, (see also the 1980 copy of the 1914 article on the same theme, edited by the Society for Christian/Jewish Cooperaticn, Essen)
Bar- and Bat-Mitzvah in the synagogue, 1920–1937

Newspaper Articles on Talks and other Events in the Synagogue:
Are their secret Jewish Teachings? 1930
Salomon Samuel: Religious Lecture for Members of all Confessions, 1924
Jewish book of ethics, 1930
Cabbalah, 1930
Sexual hygiene amongst Jews, 1930
Rabbi Samuel's 25th anniversary, 1919
Photos of the Rabbis, Salomon Samuel, Hugo Hahn, Emil Bernhard Cohn and Paul Lazarus
Roll of Honour for fallen comrades, 1924
Pray for Victory, 1914
Today's day of prayer in Essen. Service of the Synagogue community, 1914
Heroes' memorial service, 1919
Rabbi Paul Lazarus as a Field Rabbi, 1917
Military tribute 3.1.1919
Literary Donation for Jewish Combatants, 1919

Anti-Semitic attacks:
Articles on the defilements of the synagogue between 1926 and 1932: "A Document of Shame", "Anti-Semitic Heroes in the Synagogue", "Disturbance in the Prayer Room", "Synagogue Defilements in the Rhineland", Anti-Semitic Defacements on the Synagogue, Denigration of Professor Körner for being a Jew

The synagogue in use:
Advert for service times 1937; 1938, Kantor Graf in the synagogue; renting seats, 1924; seat reservations, 1936/37; Order of Service for Feast Days, 1936; song texts for the choir at Rosh ha-Shanah and Yom Kippur, 1927
Rabbi Samuel's daughter Eva: Reminiscences of the services in the Essen synagogue, 1979
Photo of the Rabbi's son, Hans Samuel at the synagogue organ
Report on the dress rehearsal of the synagogue choirs from Essen and Düsseldorf for the Jewish Winter Aid, 1937; January 1938
Weekday synagogue. Photo of the interior: handover to the Eastern Jewish Benefit Society, August 1919

Misuse during the Second World War 1939–1945:
The former synagogue as an air raid shelter and fire training area, November 1940
Plan on the use of the forecourt as a fire training area for the Reich Air Protection Corps, February 1940

Post-war community:
Photos: the ruins of the Essen inner city area in 1945; the synagogue and the Old Catholic Church of Peace, 1945
City centre, 1949; a side view of the burnt out synagogue in the Steeler Straße, 1945; the synagogue interior; Torah ark in 1949; newspaper article on disrepair, 1950; the Jewish community wants its synagogue restored, 1952; Police in the Traffic Office, 1952; Hazards to passers-by from falling stones.
A Sukkah in the ruined synagogue, 1948
Prayer room in the Rabbi's house, 1953/54
Community office, 1953/54
Lounge, 1953/54
Sarcophagus in front of the Essen synagogue, 1949
Memorial plaque, 1961
Memo from the city archives on commemorative inscriptions, 1945–1961

House of Industrial Design 1960–1979:
What is the city going to do with the synagogue it has bought? From the Ruhrnachrichten, 15.9.1959
Sales agreement between the Jewish Trust Corporation and the city of Essen, 20.10.1959
Photos of the main room being converted into a House of Industrial Design. Scaffolding for hanging the ceiling
Four photos: the synagogue shortly before the completion of rebuilding work in May 1961
The Rabbi's house from the east, 1960
Article in the Essener Zeitung, 3.3.1961
"Synagogue to be exhibition space. A worthy use for the former synagogue in Essen". In the Allgemeine Wochenzeitung der Juden in Deutschland, 3.3.1961
Six photos on the House of Industrial Design ("Haus Industrieform") between 1961 and 1970
Poster for the opening of the Poster Museum, post-1970 (new: "House of Industrial Design" and Poster Museum)
Opening event, 29.10.1970
Photo: interior of the House of Industrial Design, 1970

Newspaper cutting. Opinions on the House of Industrial Design, Essen's former synagogue. From the Allgemeine Wochenzeitung der Juden in Deutschland , 22.11.1963
Text from F. A. Reinhardt / C. Wanninger: Die rote Linie, Ludwigsburg 2004/2005, p. 48 f.

Further reading:
Heinrich Theodor Grütter (ed.): Vom Haus Industrieform zum Red Dot Design Museum. Eine Essener Designgeschichte, Essen 2015, pp. 36–55.

Memorial site 1980–2007:
Memorandum from the Society for Christian/Jewish Cooperation, 1981
Photos:
View of the main room. Opening 9.11.1980
View of the foyer
View of the exhibition

History of the Building:
Newspaper article, March 1980
Telegram from Rabbi Henry I. Szobel to the Lord Mayor of Essen, 17.12.1980
The conscience of the city for the last five years: from the Neue Ruhr Zeitung (NRZ), 9.11.1985
Securing evidence at the Old Synagogue: from the NRZ, 27.7.1985
A lot more was destroyed after 1945: from the NRZ, 6.9.1986

"Resistance and Persecution" exhibition:
Photos of the main area, central installation: Aryan bench and photos of murdered Jews

Reconstruction 1986–1988:
Torah shrine
Tracery on the window in Steeler Straße
Excerpt from the speech given by Anna Ranasinghe at the re-opening of the Old Synagogue in 1988
Photo exhibition "Stations of Jewish Life"
"A building for God and the world. The finest synagogue in Europe is 75 years old": from NRZ, 25.9.1988
"A look through the backgrounds", from: NRZ 21.9.1991
Temporary exhibition: Hanna Arendt. The life history of a German Jew, 1995
Temporary exhibition: State Security. Guaranteeing the SED Dictatorship, 13.3.1997–13.4.1997:
Photo: Joachim Gauck and Edna Brocke
Temporary exhibition: Israel in frames. Impressions, 15.5.1998–7.9.1998
"Police protection for the Old Synagogue. Two attacks in two days". From: WAZ (=Westdeutsche Allgemeine Zeitung), 2.3.1994
"Fears of fresh violence. Fury at violence after protests". From: WAZ, 9.10.2000
"Prison sentences after shots in front of the Old Synagogue". From: NRZ, 5.4.2001
Essays and photos on events between 5th November 2002 and 2007

House of Jewish Culture (Ideas 2001–2003):
"Essen's synagogue to be a Jewish museum": WAZ, 14.2.2001
"A terrifying amount of ignorance amongst young people": WAZ, 14.2.2001
"Jewish Life": WAZ, 27.10.2001
"New expert plans for the Old Synagogue": WAZ, 27.10.2001
"Not a museum but a building for the future": NRZ, 27.10.2001
"In three steps to the decoration": NRZ, 3.4.2003

Design competition 2005/06:
Presentation of the prize-winners, 2006
"Competition for the Old Synagogue": WAZ, 20.8.2005
"New ideas for the Old Synagogue": WAZ, 24.3.2006

Rebuilding/Reopening 2009/10:
School students painting the building fence, 2009
A view from the scaffolding into the main room
Excerpt from the decision of the council of the city of Essen, 27.2.2008
"Politicians give the go-ahead for the Old Synagogue": NRZ, 27.2.2008
"Don't keep harking back to the past": NRZ, 17.10.2008
"A woman and her life work": WAZ, 15.5.2010
Photos of the re-opening, dancers and musicians on 13.7.2010

The sarcophagus dominating the entrance to the building after the war (until 2008)

A view of the *Jewish Way of Life* section with the film pillar and glass cases showing Jewish sports and yoga

Jewish Way of Life

Inscription:

Contrary to widespread opinion Jewishness is much more than religion, and cannot be summed up alone with the idea of a religious community. Jewishness is an all-embracing life culture, which equally comprises diversity, differences and connecting elements. Above all Jewishness has nothing to do with the everyday clichés that exist about it.

The section of the exhibition entitled *The Jewish Way of Life* invites visitors to enjoy some unusual insights into Jewish life. How does this way of life express itself in music, videos and films, dance and clothing, in social and sporting organisations, in the media etc, etc. These are only a few areas of life that are covered in this section. You'll be guaranteed a few surprises, and a lot of humour.

Concept:
Jüdische Kulturagentur Esther Graf-Haber, Tatjana Altenburg Mannheim/Heidelberg

Installations:
A wooden wheel with the Hebrew Alefbeit (Alphabet) and Hebrew expressions in German slang
Sport movements (Torah Yoga, Maccabiade, Krav Maga (contact wrestling)
Three pillars with film and YouTube excerpts:
- „Alles auf Zucker", Dani Levy, 2004
- Rashevski's Tango, Philippe Blasband, 2004
- Yentl, Barbara Streisand, 1983

Ballet room installation with Israeli folk dances, music and spoken guidance
A touch table in the middle of the room helps you to find out more about Jewish centres in major cities. It provides a brief survey of the number, history and languages of Jewish groups. There follow symbols which can be clicked on for synagogues, kosher restaurants or shops, cultural centres and social meeting points (as of 2010). Most of these are illustrated with photos.
The cities are:
- Antwerp
- Berlin
- Buenos Aires
- Cape Town
- London
- Melbourne
- Moscow
- New York
- Teheran
- Tel Aviv (all researched by Katharina Vollus, art and com, Berlin 2010)

The "touch table" enables visitors to research ten larger Jewish communities throughout the world, including Cape Town, Melbourne, Teheran, Tel Aviv, London and Antwerp

Video corner. Persons form Germany and Israel speaking on their own Jewish identity and their relationship to Jewish life in Germany

Jewish Way of Life

Since the late Middle Ages Hebraisms have found their way into German slang used by travelling people and thieves via Western Yiddish

Dance installation, Israeli folk dances are popular among folk music lovers in Europe

Jewish Identities Today

In the area of religion three modern currents began to distinguish themselves from one another in the 1840s: modern orthodox (later, a minority), conservative and liberal. In the second half of the 19th century secularisation began to spread amongst Jews in Western Europe. This led to the so-called "Three Day Jewishness" phenomenon, i.e. as with many Christians in churches, people only visited the synagogue on two or three specific days a year for Jewish rites like circumcision, Bar-Mitzvah, weddings and funerals, but not more. Around 1900 people increasingly began to contravene the laws governing food, religious days of rest and holy days. Social control put a brake on this process in Jewish rural communities, but in large urban centres this was more and more widespread, as witnessed by many memoirs.

Relationships between the tendencies stayed somewhat more traditional in Eastern Europe. Here Orthodox Judaism retained its relatively strong position in religious communities. Nonetheless secular movements grew up amongst Polish and Russian Jews in the 1890s. The General Jewish Workers' Federation had a modern, rather secular identity on the basis of Yiddish, and fought for national minority rights. The Federation was socialist in outlook. The Zionist world movement, founded in 1897, which had many supporters amongst Eastern European Jews, also had a secular outlook. Up to the 1920s it tended to split into two camps: socialist and middle-class nationalist. Orthodox Judaism had declined in importance. Nonetheless in Eastern Europe there were scarcely any other religious tendencies. Liberal and Conservative Jewish groups were still small.

Around 1750 orthodox Jews split into Lithuanian and Hasidic persuasions. The Mussar movement sprang up amongst Lithuanian Jews who were intellectual and more orientated towards ethics, whilst Hasidic Judaism was more shot through with ecstatically emotional experiences. Its adherents organised themselves into rabbinical dynasties with their own "courts" and individual groupings like the Belzer, Satmarer and Czortkov Hasidim, many of whom managed to flee to Western Europe (Antwerp, London), the USA (Brooklyn) and Palestine (Mea Shearim, Bnei Brak) before 1939.

Secular Jews tended to meet up in cultural clubs, and Jewish periodicals were set up. Political movements had their own weeklies with plenty of choice according to orientation.

At the same time there was an enormous amount of immigration between 1880 and 1939. A large majority of Eastern European Jews saw no future in their own countries and immigrated to the USA, South America, South Africa and Australia. A small proportion also immigrated to Palestine, which was under British administration. Here a modern Jewish community began to grow up, that attracted a lot of inner-Jewish attention in the 1920s and 1930s. Zionism aimed at creating a new "Hebrew person", the "Haluz" or "pioneer", dedicated to physical work in the countryside in order to make the land of their forefathers fruitful.

The Zionist movement grew into a self-confident and, where necessary, resistant form of Judaism

But alongside this a new modern "Hebrew city" called Tel Aviv was created. Its inhabitants adopted a great deal of modern European cultural attitudes, and many buildings were built in the Bauhaus style between the end of the 1920s and the 1930s. Around 430,000 Jews lived in Palestine in the 1930s, less than 3% of the Jewish population in the world that was around 16,000,000 at the time.

The mass murder of European Jews all but destroyed Jewish life. In 1947 there were estimated to be around 4,400,000 survivors. By 2011 this number had shrunk to around 1,400,000 because of immigration and ageing. Today around 5,500,000 Jews live in each of the major Jewish centres of the world, the USA and Israel.

Old Synagogue Essen – House of Jewish Culture

Reactions to the Shoah, the mass murder of the European Jews, will affect Jewish identity for many years to come. Threats of terrorism from various different political directions – from near East terrorism to extreme left-wing and neo-Nazi attacks – also continue to affect Jewish life. In the past forty years attitudes towards Jews have also deteriorated in France, the largest Jewish community in Western Europe. As a result there has been a considerable rise in emigration to Israel. In France the attackers often have an Arab (Maghreb) background: they attack French Jews as a sign of their solidarity with the inhabitants of Palestine. Setting fire to prayer rooms, desecrating Jewish cemeteries, physical attacks on religious Jews, both men and women, and on kosher supermarkets are terrifyingly common events. It is still impossible to predict what effect such outrages will have on the future.

For current news, see the websites of Jewish news magazines and the café in the foyer:
Jüdische Allgemeine (Berlin, founded in 1946 in Düsseldorf as the "Jewish Community Paper for the North Province"): http://www.juedische-allgemeine.de/
The Jewish Chronicle (London): http://www.thejc.com/
Actualité Juive (Paris): http://www.actuj.com/
"tachles" (Zürich 2000ff.): http://www.tachles.ch/
"wina". the Jewish city magazine (Vienna 2011 ff.): http://www.wina-magazin.at/

Glass case with clothing:
Hulza khula, "blue (worker's) shirt": left-wing Zionist Youth Federation Hashomer Hatzair (= Young Guards), Vienna (founded in 1914 in the tradition of the German "Wandervogel" movement and the English Boy Scouts)
Historic officiating gown for a cantor, Germany
Kitchen apron with a slogan "Jewlicious", and references to religious dishes, Diverse Jewish accessories (good luck charms, domestic charms, small identification symbols like key rings etc.)
Hasidic costume: long black coat with a fur hat (Streimel or Spodik)
Superman symbol with the Star of David
Several kippot (caps for boys)

Kashrut (Jewish religious dietary laws):
Here you will find a glass case with a conveyor belt. Press the red knob and it will show you examples of Kosher food and non-Kosher animals, milky, fleshy, parve (= neutral), Passover food, Shabbat food. Explanations are provided on the monitor.

The variety of Jewish identities can be seen from the clothing: all the way from the Hashomer Hatzair Young People's Socialist Federation in Vienna to ultra-orthodox Hasidic garments, a frock coat and a "shtreimel" (fur hat), made in 18th century Poland

News magazines are important for strengthening Jewish identities. Almost every Jewish group has one. The websites of Jewish societies are also presented on the touch screen

Old Synagogue Essen – House of Jewish Culture

Kashrut – Jewish religious dietary laws

Jewish eating traditions started in Biblical times to distinguish their diets from those of surrounding heathen cultures. Thus wine had to be produced under Jewish control, since naked men and women paid homage to the god Bacchus by dancing when they stamped the grapes to mash (the so-called "bacchanalia"). Jews were forbidden to drink any such wine made in this manner.

Any form of cruelty had to be avoided. Hence a young lamb would not be cooked in its mother's milk, as was apparently common in other cults in the Near East in ancient times. (2nd Book of Moses 23, 19 ff.; 3rd Book of Moses 11, 29 f., 43–45; 5th Book of Moses 14, 3, 19, 21). The dietary laws were announced in the Torah without giving any reasons. People attempted to justify them later during the Enlightenment. The ban on eating pork was often traced back to the poor storage conditions that gave rise to trichina worms. But there is no mention of this in the text.

The dietary laws became even more difficult in the Rabbinic age. Now the ban on cooking lamb in its mother's milk was extended to include a strict separation between "milk" and "meat" dishes (the Babylonian Talmud Tract Hulin, fol. 115b). Depending on where they lived, people were expected to wait 4 to 5 hours between consuming meat and milk dishes, and one hour between eating milk and meat dishes. Different plates, cutlery, pots and kitchen instruments were used. Jewish religious traditions were expected to be complied with in everyday life, and not simply remain "spiritual".

Hellenistic Jews were one of the first groups to register doubts about rigorously interpreting the dietary laws. Early Christians took up these objections and abolished them for Christians of non-Jewish origin.

The upshot was that Jewish groups began to develop slightly different eating traditions. After their persecution during the Crusades in 1096, Ashkenazi (Central European) rabbis issued decrees forbidding their followers to eat pulses during Pessach (the Passover), the holiday recalling the liberation of the Jews from Egypt. Sephardic (Spanish-Andalusian) Jews refused to go along with this and still eat rice and peas today. Yemenite Jews did not regard poultry as "meat", but as "neutral". Although locusts were regarded in the Bible as "impure", pragmatic Moroccan rabbis allowed them to be eaten in the Atlas Mountains because they were the only source of protein.

Islam has adopted some of the Jewish dietary laws, like the ban on eating pork and the particular form of slaughtering animals. Here the idea is to leave as little blood in the meat as possible since this is the "seat of the soul" and blood should not be consumed where possible (3rd Book of Moses 3,17; 17, 10ff.). That said, Islam does not separate milk and meat dishes, and Sunni Muslims at least allow the consumption of seafood.

Jews in different countries have adopted their local eating customs to include kosher variations. Italian Jews, for example, have developed tasty cold pasta sauces for Shabbat when it is forbidden to light fires.

The dietary laws were broadly observed until the mid-19th century. But in German-speaking countries this declined as West European Jews became more urbane, and emigration from small rural communities into large cities increased after the 1860s. True, Jewish community institutions continued to observe them but by the start of the First World War this only applied to around 10% to 15% of German-speaking Jews. Polish and Sephardic (North African and Near Eastern) Jews were, however, more conservative.

There were – and still are – many hybrid forms. A large number of Jews do not eat pork, seafood and forbidden fish (i.e. those with skin like sharks, eels and swordfish), but they do eat meat that has not been slaughtered in a kosher manner. Many people cook typical Jewish dishes, like Central European Jews during Pessach who eat matzo dumplings made from unleavened flour. Some keep the Passover plates used by their ancestors and use them during this holiday. Others recall typical Shabbat dishes like Tchulent or Schalet. One of these was the German poet Heinrich Heine, who was brought up in a traditional Jewish family and could even read the letters written by his mother in German/Jewish handwriting. Under "Princess Shabbat", one of the Hebrew melodies in his volume of poems "Romanzero", we read the following:

Schalet, ray of light immortal!
Schalet, daughter of Elysium!"
So had Schiller's song resounded,
Had he ever tasted schalet,

For this schalet is the very
Food of heaven, which, on Sinai,
God Himself instructed Moses
In the secret of preparing,

At the time He also taught him
And revealed in flames of lightning
All the doctrines good and pious,
And the holy Ten Commandments.

Yes, this schalet's pure ambrosia
Of the true and only God:
Paradisal bread of rapture

Translation by Margaret Armour (1860–1943)

Jewish cooking course are very popular and, not least because of non-Jewish interest, there are a lot of German books on different types of Jewish dishes. Eating is one way of defining your identity. But in everyday life many Jews are aggravated by their dietary restrictions. Jews who are faithful to traditional restriction can only accept invitations to meals under certain conditions. It is possible to eat fish and salads but glass plates can only be used if they have no pores.

The Conference of Orthodox Rabbis in Germany (ORD) has an internet page showing the current list of kosher food.

There is a huge range of observances. In this respect Jews in Germany are particularly worldly in comparison with their counterparts in France and Switzerland. There are scarcely any kosher restaurants in major German cities. Instead restaurants tend to offer "kosher-style" dishes, modelled on American patterns. They can thus avoid having to pay for the necessary rabbinical supervision, whilst using only kosher ingredients and opening on Saturdays to attract more customers on their day off.

Kosher in NRW (2016):
Wuppertal: Café Negev, (Gemarker Straße 15, 42275 Wuppertal.
    Open, Monday to Thursday 11.30–20.00; Fridays 10.00–17.30 (summer)
Cologne: there is a Kosher canteen in the synagogue community,
Düsseldorf: the community supports a kosher food shop named "Kosher King",
    Bankstraße 71, 40476 Düsseldorf
www.nicht-mit-uns.com/Geschaefte.htm
www.jgd.de/judentum/kaschrut

Kosher-style:
Bochum: "Matzen" Restaurant, Erich-Mendel Platz 1, 44791 Bochum,
    www.matzen-restaurant.de
Düsseldorf: "Die Kurve", Goebenstraße 18, 40477 Düsseldorf, www.die-kurve.com/
Düsseldorf: "Rimon", Weseler Straße 53, 40239 Düsseldorf,
    Sundays to Thursdays 3–9 pm, Fridays 11 am–3 pm

Further reading:
Marlena Spieler, the jewish heritage cookbook, a fascinating journey through the rich
    and diverse history of the Jewish cuisine, London 2002
Anat Helman (ed.), Jews and their foodways, New York 2015
Rachel Heuberger/Regina Schneider, Koscher Style: 80 köstliche Rezepte aus der
    Jüdischen Küche, München 2004
Tuvia Hod / Yzchak Ehrenberg, Rabbi, ist das koscher?: der Ratgeber, wie Sie sich in
    Deutschland koscher ernähren können, edited by the Orthodox Rabbi Conference
    Germany with the support of the Central Council of Jews in Germany and the
    World Zionist Organisation, Cologne 2010 (5010)
Saul Wagschal, A practical guide to kashruth, 2003
Website ORD: http://www.ordonline.de/koscherliste

The traditional dietary rules are explained on a monitor showing objects and texts

Texts on the screens of the kashrut unit:

Kosher means "fit", "proper" or "ritually pure". It covers many areas in life, but is mostly known in connection with food and drink. Even religious Jews love almost every sort of food and sweets. But in order for them to be able to enjoy them freely they have to be checked by Rabbis and declared to be "kosher". Kosher certificates can be found in certain restaurants and on packings in the form of printed symbols. Every year the Conference of Orthodox Rabbis in Germany publishes a list of kosher products offered in Germany.

....

Parve means "neutral". All products that contain neither meat nor milk are designated as "parve". These include flour, eggs, fruit, vegetables, cereals, plant oils, nuts, coffee, sugar, syrup, honey, cocoa, tea and water.

Fish is regarded as kosher, so long as it has scales and fins it is equally parve. All other seafood is, according to the Torah, not kosher. (3rd Book of Moses 11 and 5, and Moses 14, 3–21)

Before eating their food very orthodox Jews take care to see it is free of insects. Parve products can be cooked and eaten with milk and meat products alike.

Old Synagogue Essen – House of Jewish Culture

„Thou shalt not seethe a kid in his mother's milk" (2nd Book of Moses 23,19)
This clear instruction is repeated three times in the Tora. In mediaeval times people interpreted this to mean that food containing meat and milk should be kept separate from one another. A cheeseburger and spaghetti Bolognese with parmesan cheese are therefore not kosher.

This custom was extended to including kitchen utensils. In a kosher kitchen they are optically and spatially separated into "milk" and "meat". This instruction, like the others, is consciously ignored by many Jews.

....

The Torah lists kosher animals. (3rd Book of Moses 11 and 5th Book of Moses 14, 3–21). The most popular are beef, veal, goat, mutton, lamb, chicken and turkey. Pork and donkey meat are not kosher.

To ensure that meat is kosher animals have to be slaughtered in a special way, known as "shechitah".

A "shochet" (the man who performs the "shechitah") must be Jewish and properly trained. He uses a particularly sharp knife because the trachea and oesophaguos have to be severed in a single cut. A second cut is forbidden, as is any form of anaesthetic. An animal killed by hunting is not regarded as kosher. The "shechitah" and exsanguination are followed by an inspection of the meat. After eating meat dishes religious Jews wait several hours before they eat milk dishes. Thus they desist from putting milk in coffee directly after a kosher schnitzel.

....

You can find identical food in many Jewish households all over the world This is an expression of a Jewish culinary style, a mixture of oriental and Eastern European traditions, refined with products from Israel.

Alongside Jewish recipes in books by Jamie Oliver and Tim Melzer, Jewish cookbooks also contain kosher recipes. These will tell you how to prepare traditional dishes like gefilte fish and Matzah ball soup and more contemporary dishes like sushi with kosher fish.

....

There are two separate areas in a kosher kitchen: one for meat products that is traditionally marked in red; and one for milk products that is marked blue. Each area has its own utensils, plates, glasses and cutlery in order to avoid mixing them. In a refrigerator or freezer they can be placed next to each other because the decisive factor is the cooled state.

Separate sinks and washing machines are necessary in a kosher kitchen. For this reason every large Jewish kitchen has two separate rooms. This also explains why many kosher catering establishment either offer fish or milk dishes.

Many Jewish families start the weekly day of rest with a festive meal. Before they begin to eat the wine is blessed aloud, followed by the bread, two braided loaves, called "hallot" (plural of hallah). In towns with large Jewish communities you can buy freshly baked "hallot" in kosher bakeries.

A favourite hors d'oeuvres in Eastern European Jewish dishes is gefilte fish (ground carp mixed and shaped into patties). The favourite main course is meat and stewed fruit is served as dessert.

On Shabbat itself (a Saturday) there is a festive lunch.

The ban on working during Shabbat was defined by rabbis very early on, but it is only observed by a minority of Jews. At the same time many families continue to uphold the custom of gathering to eat lunch on Shabbat together.

....

An eight-day holiday, Pessach (Passover) recalls the flight of the Israelis from Egypt. The sudden exodus from the land of slavery left no time for their bread to leaven. In memory of this the Torah (5th Book of Moses 16, 3) commands believers not to eat leavened bread for seven days. This means all food containing cereals (bread, noodles and dishes with flour), rice and pulses.

The Pessach holiday bread, Matzo, is unleavened. The dough consists of water and wheat flour and is unleavened because it is kneaded and baked within 18 minutes. Wine is offered during Pessach as with every meal on a Jewish holiday: but during Pessach it must be kosher wine. This means that the Rabbi who oversees the production of the wine must ensure that the fermented grape juice conforms to all the dietary laws for Pessach. Pessach is the holiday most celebrated by Jews all over the world.

....

The opposite of kosher (ritually pure) – terefah (ritually impure) – exists only in relationship to food and drink. The Torah (3rd Book of Moses 11,41) states that "... every creeping thing that creepeth upon the earth shall be an abomination; it shall not be eaten". This applies, amongst others, to marine animals and seafood like lobsters, crabs, oysters, as well as insects and worms. This is why orthodox Jews take great care to clean vegetables, in order to ensure they contain no insects and grubs. The rule is: if it comes from something pure, it is pure. Thus milk from impure cattle and game like donkey milk, the eggs and offspring of impure birds, and the roe of impure fish (like caviar from sturgeon) are all forbidden. Thus non-kosher animals like pigs and horses are regarded as terefah.

A Jewish joke goes as follows: "Why does a Jew have three refrigerators? That's obvious. One for meat, one for milk products and one for terefah!"

"The dietary laws train us to master our appetites. The object of all these laws is to restrain the growth of desire, the indulgence in seeking that which is pleasant, and the disposition to consider the appetite for eating and drinking as the end (of man's existence). (Maimonides, The Guide for the Perplexed)

For those who consciously follow the food laws and the instructions on how to conduct a kosher household it is often more about expressing their own Jewish identity than simply preserving a tradition. These eating habits known as the kosher lifestyle are very popular in many large cities. Some restaurants offer Jews the opportunity to keep up this way of life outside their own homes.

Audio corner:
Music and songs by Jewish musicians: Naomi Shemer: Jerusalem of Gold. Ilan & Ilanit (* 1947, Israel's entrants in the Eurovision song contest). Milk and Honey: "Halleluja" (winning Eurovision song), Eitan Masuri, Daliah Lavi (German pop music from the 1960s, *1942). Ofra Haza (1957–2000, "im nin`alu". Yemenite-Jewish music). Matisjahu (* 1979, Matthew Paul Miller, former Orthodox rapper from America). Esther and Abi Ofarim: German hits. Georg Kreisler (19222011, cabaret artist, migrant returnee, Vienna). Avishai Cohen: Sephardic song ("Morenica"). Arik Einstein (1939–2013). Chava Alberstein: Yiddish song, "Hadag Nachasch". Dudu (David) Fischer (*1951). Esther (*1941) and Abi Ofarim (*1937): Cinderella Rockefella. Shtreiml: Fishelach in vasser. Pharao's daughter: "Im ein ani li, mi li". Anakronic Electro orchestra: Free clarinet screaming my head, "Eize medina" ("Which state", singer unknown)

Video corner (on the right):
Three monitors: Brief interviews with Jewish persons from Germany and Israel: incl. Julian Chaim Soussan, former Rabbi in Düsseldorf (2010), now in Frankfurt; Herbert Rubinstein, Düsseldorf. Questions include their attitude to the Jewish religion, on "Jewishness", "Being a Jew", on the State of Israel, on Jewish life in Germany etc.

Installation (in the centre on the left):
A private library of anonymous Jewish persons around the whole world. The installation reveals utterly different interests. They also include books in common.
Dan, 60, China; Joseph, 33, Bulgaria; Hannah, 70, Israel; Irina 21, Russia; Eli 60, Netherlands; Carl 56 , Canada; Mirjam 43, Hungary; Noa and Nelly, 10 and 7, Germany ; Sami 33, Turkey; Jenny, 57, USA; Susanna, 64, Argentina; Noam, 9, Israel.

Audio corner

Installation of private Jewish libraries world wide

Old Synagogue Essen – House of Jewish Culture 189

History of the Jewish Community in Essen

Inscription:

The first written mention of Jews in Essen was in a document dating back to 1291. But it was only after the onset of industrialisation towards the end of the end of the 19th century that the Jewish community (like the rest of the Essen) grew considerably. By 1933 the Jewish community, which numbered around 5,000, contributed to the cultural, social and economic life of the city. Around 2,500 Jews from Essen were murdered in the Shoah. Others survived by fleeing the city and emigrating.

The wearisome rebuilding of a new Jewish community, predominantly made up of Eastern European refugees, shortly after the Second World War no longer took place in the destroyed synagogue in Essen but in the neighbouring house that once belonged to the Rabbi. In 1959 the Jewish Cultural Community in Essen opened its new synagogue in a Sedanstraße. Since then this has been the headquarters of Jewish life as it is practised here. The former synagogue building and the Rabbi's house have passed into the ownership of the city of Essen.

The exhibition section entitled *History of the Jewish Community in Essen* tells of Jewish life in Essen, concentrating on the end of the 19th century and the first half of the 20th century. Its exhibits reveal moving stories: they include personal objects like poetry albums, photos, diaries of flight, testimonies, certificates and medals from the life of Jews from Essen, also from those who immigrated to other countries.

Particular attention is dedicated to the family of Rabbi Samuel. There is also a reading corner containing publications from the first decades of the 20th century. If you wish to delve deeper into the subject there is a touch station with screens that contains a huge number of systematically arranged documents to help you investigate Jewish history in Essen.

Jewish families in Essen:

Hans Winter (1911–1999): Leisure diary (AR 3337)
Photos: Hans Winter with friends, ca 1930 (AR 4974)
The Jewish Youth Club in Essen, ca 1930 (without an AR no.)
Hans Winter in Essen, 1986

Dispatch book recording the wedding of Mathilde Herz and Bernhard Wielens in 1896 (Inv. no. 080). Photo (AR 9836)

Letter of congratulation on the wedding anniversary of Julius and Martha Hellendahl 1915: (AR 8177)

Letter written by children on Rosh ha-Shanah 1887 (AR 8174)

Photo taken on the birthday of Johann Rindskopf 1911: (AR 3142)

The Jewish sports club "Hakoah" (= "Strength"), founded in 1923, Jakob Margolies, certificate 1931 3rd place 100 metres (AR 1278)
Photo (AR 1265)

The goalkeeper in the Jewish sports club, Werner Storch, 1926. Photo (AR 10555)

Associate Judge Hugo Stern (1889–1958) (AR 3645), Hugo Stern in the trainee's club "Haselmaus" in Bochum 1913 (AR 5151), Hugo Stern in the Poseidon canoe club, Essen 1929 (AR 5159). Hugo Stern with his son Heinrich on the Ruhr 1931

Report book and class photo of the Jewish school, Inge Sachs (born 1923) (AR 7578). The report book is opened on the page for 1937. Photo (AR 7574)

Invitation to the centenary celebration in the main hall of the Jewish school in Sachsenstraße on the 12th July 1930. (AR 8589)
Song text (AR 8591)

Alex Marx from Essen (1894–1981) immigrated to Palestine in 1938 and later moved to the USA.
War Ration Book, AR 8604). Identity Card (AR 8601). Alex Marx's passport, issued by the British Mandate Government in Palestine 1938.

Iwan Guggenheim (1914–1999)
Guggenheim fled from Essen in 1938 and immigrated to Palestine via Switzerland and Italy. In 1958 he returned to Essen as one of the few survivors.
The diary of his flight (AR 0245)
Photo (AR 1449): Guggenheim and his wife as an event held by the Jewish community in Essen, ca. 1959
Photo (Inv. no. 138): Iwan Guggenheim 1989

Erich Sternberg from Essen was already in Cuba when he wrote to his sister about his wife's failed attempt to flee to Cuba aboard the "St Louis" in 1939. Despite being transported back to Europe his wife was able to save herself and rejoined her husband in the USA in 1940.
Letter (AR 0916)

After studying at the Jewish school, Werner Gans (1914–1989) went into his parents trading business and fled to South Africa in 1936. A woman friend of the family who managed to reach Brazil wrote to him about his parents in Essen. In South Africa he married a Czech Jewish woman.
An excuse note to the Jewish school in Essen, and an essay, 1920/21 (AR 10467)
Letter and poem (AR 7337)
Letter 1940 (AR 7336)
Wedding invitation (AR 1457)

Ilse Heide, married name Dorfzaun (1928–2005), fled to Ecuador in 1941 where she married into a hat-making family.
Panama hats. Picture on the Internet page of the K business (no number)
Panama hat (AR 4963)
The Heide family in Columbia (AR 9684)

Martin Stern (born 1924) had an adventurous flight to the USA via Italy, France and North Africa.
Emigration account (AR 9441)
Photo (AR 9206): The siblings Annelore, Henry, Martin and Frank Stern (l. to r.) in the USA, 1944

The section on the *History of the Jewish Community in Essen*, here presenting the Jewish infrastructure in the 1920s and 1930s

The only reconstructed stained-glass window shows the seven-armed candlestick (Menorah) in the West facade

Martha Simon (born 1896) was a member of the Red Cross in Steele and head shopkeeper in her husband's clothing and haberdashery business. In 1933 they fled to the Netherlands, and from there, via Belgium to Brazil in 1936. There her husband found it very difficult to establish a business.
Photo (AR 3314): Martha Simon in Red Cross uniform during the First World War.
Medal and certificate. Inv. no. 102
Photo (AR 10014): The Simon family on the crossing to Brazil in 1936

Rabbi Paul Lazarus was, from 1914–1916, the second city Rabbi alongside Salomon Samuel, as well as researching into German-Jewish history. After 1916 he was a military Rabbi in Macedonia. In 1939 he emigrated from Wiesbaden to Haifa, where he died in 1952.
Photo (AR 4004)

Further reading:
Sabine Hank, Hermann Simon, Uwe Hank, Feldrabbiner in den deutschen Streitkräften
    des Ersten Weltkrieges, Berlin 2013
Katrin Nele Jansen, Biographisches Handbuch der Rabbiner, ed. Michael Brocke, part 2,
    Die Rabbiner im Deutschen Reich 1871–1945, München 2009, p. 396 f.

Conrad Leyser (1878–1952) was a wholesale timber merchant in Essen and served in France during the First World War. After 1919 he set up the local section of the Reichsbund for Jewish Front Soldiers (RjF). In 1939 he fled to South Africa.
Certificate (AR 2175)
Military pass with credentials (AR 7319). Certificate of good conduct for private
    Conrad Leyser 1898
Photo (AR 3725): David and Conrad Leyser in the field in France, 1914/18

Siegfried Blum (1906–1976) lived in the Essen suburb of Karnap. After 1933 he fled to Holland. In 1940 he was arrested and interned in the concentration camp in Westerbork. As one of the few survivors he immigrated to Great Britain in 1945.
Camp ID (AR 0927)
Congratulations to Siegfried Blum from his fellow prisoners in Westerbork, 1942 (AR 2072)

Selma Krieger (born 1923) wrote a letter to two friends in England in 1939. She was deported on 27th October 1941 and murdered.
Letter (AR 0997)
Photo (AR 1661): The three friends in a group of young Jews, 1937

Doris Lissauer, maiden name Moses (born 1926), saved some small remains from the ruins of the interior of the synagogue on the 10th November 1938. After fleeing to the Netherlands she was deported to the concentration camp in Westerbork. She was one of the few survivors and immigrated to Australia.
Poetry album (AR 1058, 1059)
Photo (AR 3784): Doris Moses, her parents and brother shortly before immigrating to the
    Netherlands

From 27th to 28th October 1938 17 000 Jews of Polish origin were deported from Germany to the border area between Poland and the German Reich. Before that the Nazis had deprived them of their citizenship. Herschel Grynspan was so furious about this that he assassinated the German ambassador in Paris, Ernst vom Rath. Hitler used this as a pretext for the pogrom night of 9th to 10th November. After she was allowed into Poland Paula Waldhorn was able to flee to England with a "Kindertransport". She later immigrated to Israel, where she was called Penina Galili.
Large handkerchief from Zbąszyń (AR 4409)
Photo (AR 1913): Paula Waldhorn on her last day at school, together with her class in the
    Jewish school, 1937. Paula is standing in the centre of the top row. Curls, dark dress
    with a white collar.

Abraham Mühlrad was also deported to Zbąszyń where Leo Wels gave him a handkerchief painted with Indian ink. Wels was later a well-known artist in Israel, under the name Naftali Bezem. Abraham Mühlrad's family were murdered.
Small handkerchief from Zbąszyń (AR 4463)
The last photo of the Mühlrad family together before they were deported to Zbąszyń in 1938: (AR 3768). Abraham Mühlrad is standing in the front row, second from the left.

The history of the family of Rabbi Samuel Salomon:
The liberal Rabbi Salomon Samuel (1867–1942) had four children with his wife Anna (1874–1942) The children immigrated to Palestine, resp. Israel. He and his wife died in the Theresienstadt concentration camp in 1942. Their son Ludwig – later Elieser (1900–1966) – worked for his country. The second son Hans (1901–1976) had a talent for music.
The daughters Eva (1904–1989) and Edith (1907–1964) worked in art and design.

Further reading:
Salomon Samuel, in: Katrin Nele Jansen: Die Rabbiner im Deutschen Reich, vol. 2, Handbuch der Rabbi, ed. Michael Brocke, Munich 2009, pp. 535–538.
Eight photos of the Samuel family (AR 4010, 4011, 4027, 4102, 4103, 4109, 4120, 4984)
Rabbi Salomon Samuel's identity card, issued in 1924 (AR 8997)
Photo of Salomon Samuel, ca 1930 (AR 4018)
A card from Salomon Samuel congratulating Wilhelm Hollinger on his Bar-Mitzvah of 1927, with a transcription (AR 8801)
Sheet music belonging to Hans Samuel (copies) (no AR number)
Five linocuts by Eva Samuel for Jewish Festivities (AR 10432). Book by Eva Samuel, Zijurim/Paintings, 1988

Objects related to Edith Samuel:
Edith Samuel's passport, 1939 (AR 4673)
Five dolls of Jewish children in the Land of Israel (AR 4954, 4955, 4956, 4957, 49610)
Edith Samuel and Leah Goldberg, Banim Banot Bubot (Boys, girls, puppets), Tel Aviv 1968 (Hebrew) (AR 10434)
"Yakinton", a magazine of Jews in Israel who came from Central Europe, May 2009. It contains an article on Edith Samuel

Painting of Frida Levy, Ernst Levy and drawings of Edith Samuel:
Richard Friedrich Reusing (1874–1956): Frida Levy, 1907
Gift from their son Bertold Levy, Sweden
Frida Levy (1881–1942) and her husband, the lawyer Dr. Friedrich Levy (1875–1936) supported a huge number of artistic, social and political institutions and projects. They were also actively engaged in the peace and women's movement. Frida Levy remained in Germany during the Nazi period to try to help her imprisoned son-in-law. She refused to go underground to avoid putting anyone else in danger. In 1942 she was deported to Riga, where she was murdered.
Klara Herzfeld (*1879): Ernst Levy
Gift from his son Juan Levy, Argentina
Dr. Ernst Levy (1872–1945), the brother-in-law of Frida Levy, was a doctor in Essen. During the First World War he was the head of a military hospital set up by the Jewish "Glückauf" lodge. In 1939 he escaped with his wife to Argentina.
Klara Herzfeld from Essen was a talented artist. Her husband Ernst Herzfeld was the chair of the Jewish community's welfare office. After the November pogrom in 1938 they fled to Palestine.

Frida Levy fought for women's rights and had an artists' salon in Essen. She was murdered in the Shoah.

The solicitor Friedrich Levy represented many persons with left-wing views. He was high on the National Socialist list.

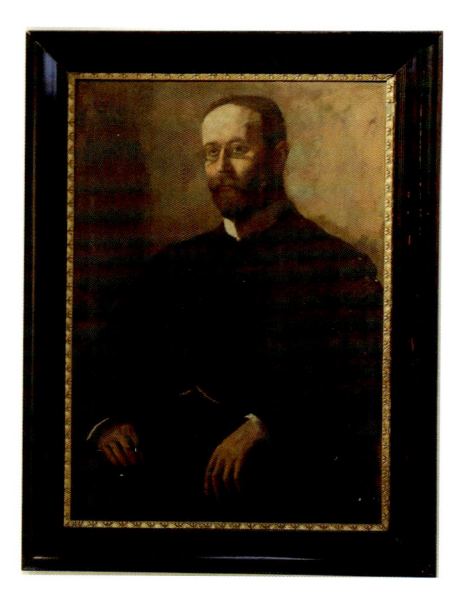

Pencil drawing by Edith Samuel, a daughter of the Rabbi Salomon Samuel, undated

Edith Samuel (1907–1964): Drawings
Edith Samuel was the youngest daughter of the Rabbi Salomon Samuel from Essen. Her immense artistic talents were already apparent as a child. She studied drawing, woodcutting and sculpture in the Folkwang Academy. However she was particularly keen on making puppets. Even today her works are still well-known in Israel.
The drawings are about making a bust.

Naftali Bezem (*1924)
Born in Essen, he was the son of the Synagogue attendant. He was deported with his family to the border of Germany and Poland at the end of October 1938. From there they immigrated to Palestine. He trained at the Bezalel Academy of Arts under the Bauhaus student Mordechai Ardon. He was a freelance artist (oil paintings, sculpture, reliefs, carpets, installations, stained glass). He made the wall relief for the Yad va-Shem place of memorial (1970) and was responsible for the painted ceilings in the President's palace.
   In this water-colour Bezem recalls his murdered parents and the Essen synagogue. (Private owner. Loaned to the Old Synagogue in Essen)

The six touch screens show 17 themes on Jewish local history with many images and text sources

Interactive Learning Centre (Texts on the screen):

The Middle Ages
The first written mention of a Jewish community in an area of Germany was in Cologne in 321 CE. During the Carolingian era (751-814) Jews were prominent amongst traders working in Southern Europe and the Orient. They were welcome in towns as farmers, handymen and merchants. As "aliens", however, they needed letters of protection from regional lords. Around the end of the 11th century (the Crusades) the relationship between Christians and Jews changed radically. Especially in times of need Jews were victims of riots. Special laws restricted where they were allowed to live.

The first written mention of Jews in Essen was in 1291. As "Jews under special protection" they were subordinate to the Abbesses who ruled the town. Hence they were compelled to pay "protection money" for rights of domicile, and to pass through a territory. Notwithstanding, between 1328 and 1648 the town council expelled Jews from within the borders of Essen on many occasions.

Christian anti-Jewish attitudes arise from passages in the New Testament that were then included in the writings of the Church fathers. Popular belief had it that Jews were guilty of acts of sacrilege and ritual murder. During the plague in 1349 Jews were accused of poisoning the water in wells: this was also the case in Essen. In the 17th and 18th century there were only around seven Jewish families in Essen.

Emancipation and "Assimilation"
The aim of emancipation was to achieve legal, social and political equality for Jews in civil society. In Europe the French Revolution prepared the way for Jewish emancipation in 1791. In 1812 Prussia issued an edict recognising Jews as citizens of the state. That said, most of the provisions in the edict were withdrawn in 1814. Jews had to wait until 1871 before receiving equal rights in the German Reich.

In return for their emancipation Jews were expected by the majority Christian population to surrender their "Jewishness". A minority of Jews allowed themselves to be baptised and, with their status as property-owners, many Jews in major urban centres strived to become accepted as a part of the educated middle class. They orientated their lives on German culture and their outlook was often nationalistic. At the same time a considerable number of them were caught between the two poles of becoming German and remaining Jewish. Organ music was introduced into many synagogues and, against tradition, German replaced Hebrew in sermons, prayers and hymns. In their wish to be recognised as equals many Jews stressed their allegiance to all things German by interpreting their Jewishness as a "confession".

This is also expressed in the new synagogue in Essen that was opened in 1913. Its design is based on Jewish traditions. At the same time it had certain similarities to church buildings. Its magnificent building in the centre of the city was only a stone's throw away from the Catholic Minster.

Social composition

The number of Jews in the Ruhr region grew in the course of industrialisation and emancipation. Whereas there were only 370 Jews registered in Essen, Steele and Werden in 1836, in 1910 this number had risen to around 3,260 in Essen and the surrounding parishes. Only a minority of Jews, particularly those who emigrated from Easter Europe, worked in factories and mines. Because Jews were traditionally strongly orientated to education, a considerable number followed academic studies and went into self-employed professions like the law and medicine. This was also because, despite enjoying equal rights, they were denied promotion in universities, the armed forces and the civil service. Many Jews in Essen were also involved in trading activities. They ranged from peddlers to respected owners of department stores. Only a few of them could be described as being wealthy.

Jewish clubs and organisations

Despite the fact that Jews enjoyed equality before the law, they continued to suffer discrimination. One of the results was the creation of Jewish organisations and societies. Some of them were engaged in political and social areas but there were also very many sports and youth clubs.

A screenshot from the touchscreens showing a soccer team of Ha-Koah Essen in the 1920s

Jewish immigrants from Eastern Europe

There was a strong wave of Jewish emigration from Eastern Europe to Germany during the first World War and this increased during the 1920s. Many Jews were brought to Germany as forced labourers during the war, or enlisted in the war economy. Others emigrated for economic reasons or fled from persecution. The "East Jews", as they were known later, at first belonged to the lower classes. They often spoke Yiddish, had very little idea of German culture and their ties had very much to do with traditional Jewish culture and customs. Only gradually did they adapt to a middle-class way of life. In 1933 "East Jews" made up around a third of all those in the synagogue community in Essen.

Social, cultural and religious differences often led to tensions between German Jews and "East Jews", mostly within the community for there were very few private contacts. The upshot in Essen was the creation of separate East Jewish clubs which set up a "Federation of East Jewish Organisations" in 1926.

Anti-Semitism

The term "anti-Semitism" was first used in 1879 in the circle of friends around the publicist, Wilhelm Marr, to describe a new form of hostility towards Jews, which was politically organised and rooted more in racism than religion. Even today anti-Semitism is a phenomenon that is continually raising its head in politics and society. Modern anti-Semitism can be linked with the long tradition of Christian hostility towards Jews. Its appearance in the last third of the 19th century can be attributed to many causes. These include middle-class fears of social dislocation and moral decay, as well as Jewish involvement in capitalism and the workers' movement.

Community institutions

By the end of the 19th century the Jewish community in Essen had increased strongly and by 1933 it had reached a total of around 4,500. Similar to the churches it maintained many institutions, including the "Israelite primary school", the kindergarten and a child-care centre in the "Henriette Hirschland House", the Rosenau convalescent home and an Old People's home with 40 places for men and women. The community's welfare office employed a nurse. It provided financial assistance, tried to find jobs, and kept a clothes room for the very poor. There were also Jewish cemeteries, and the "chevra kadisha" (holy society) that provided care for the sick and was responsible for preparing the burial of the dead.

Suburbs

Jewish institutions not only existed in the centre of Essen, but also in some suburbs and smaller parishes in the locality. Thus Jews possessed their own prayer room in Borbeck until 1913, in Werden until 1935 and in Kettwig (south of the river) until the November pogrom in 1938. Until the 1930s Jews in Steele had their own independent synagogue community and Jewish school. Jewish cemeteries can be found in Werden, Steele and Kettwig (south of the river).

The Reich Federation of Jewish Front Soldiers
Like the non-Jewish population many Jews approved of the general atmosphere of jingoism at the start of the First World War. In the hope of being completely accepted by the majority society they regarded it as a natural duty to fight for their country in the war. But these hopes were dashed as early as 1916 when the Prussian Ministry of War conducted a so-called "Jewish count": and Jews were also held responsible for defeat at the end of the war.

The Reich Federation of Jewish Front Soldiers was founded in 1919 to remember with patriotic pride the 80,000 Jewish front soldiers and the 12,000 Jews who had died. However, it became increasingly involved in countering anti-Semitic attacks amongst the general public.

Deprivation of rights and self-assertion
Hitler's appointment as Reich Chancellor was swiftly followed by a wave of measures to discriminate and exclude the Jews. On the so-called Boycott Day on 1st April 1933, SA and SS guards blocked the entrance to Jewish businesses, medical practices and solicitors' offices. In the same month Jews were removed from the civil service.

Despite the initial shock Jews continued to hope that the situation would improve. But legal and social discrimination left heavy scars. Jews were increasingly forced to sell their businesses to non-Jews – mostly below their real value. This was the case with 80% of Jewish businesses in Essen before November 1938. The livelihood of many Jewish families was destroyed.

Jewish communities soon became the local base for sticking together and helping one another. Self-help institutions arose, not only to assist people to emigrate, but also to remain in Germany. Cultural activities were intensified to strengthen their sense of self-respect and dignity.

All in all the number of members of the Jewish community in Essen declined from 4,500 in July 1933 to 1,650 in June 1939.

The "Nuremberg Laws"
The "Nuremberg Laws" of 15th September 1935 marked a new stage in the social exclusion of the Jews. They were now considered in German law as an "inferior race". The fact that every person had inalienable equal rights at birth was no longer valid. Marriages and ex-marital relationships between Jews and "Aryans" were forbidden. The most intimate areas of life were subject to snooping and denunciation. Jews were reduced to the status of "nationals" without political rights

and set apart from so-called "Reich citizens". Lawyers and bureaucrats divided people into so-called "full Jews", "half Jews", and "quarter Jews". In order to enjoy any rights at all everyone had to prove they had "pure blood". The "Nuremberg Laws" were succeeded by countless decrees, regulations and laws which constricted even the smallest details of Jewish life. For example, Jews were forbidden to visit restaurants, cinemas, theatres and swimming baths.

Expulsion and emigration

In 1933 Jews began to leave Germany progressively. At first there were only a few but as repressions increased the numbers increased. After the 1938 November pogrom this turned into a mass exodus.

Those who wanted to leave had to overcome extremely difficult hurdles. Sometimes they failed because of the entry conditions (e.g. insufficient capital), set by the country they had chosen. Nazi bureaucratic harassment and material plundering also blocked the path to freedom. Those who succeeded could count themselves lucky, although life in a strange country was often very hard.

The countries who took in most Jews were the USA, Great Britain, Argentina and the then Palestine. Around 60% of the Jews from Essen managed to flee between 1933 and 1941. Most of those who immigrated to neighbouring countries found themselves once more in the clutches of the Nazis after the outbreak of the Second World War. They were then captured and deported to concentration camps and annihilation camps.

Zbąszyń

The policies of the Polish government were also shot through with anti-Semitism. At the start of October 1938 it announced that all nationals who had lived for more than five years outside the country and failed to renew their passports in Poland within the space of one month, would be declared stateless. This was to prevent Polish Jews from returning home. The German government reacted by forcibly deporting several thousand Polish Jews, including those living in Germany (461 from Essen), to Zbąszyń on the Polish border. Because they had been deported from Germany and Poland refused to take them in, they were condemned to suffer for weeks in a no man's land under inhumane conditions. In the end, after interventions by the Jewish communities in Poland, they were allowed to enter the country.

Amongst the deported "East Jews" was a married couple from Hanover, named Grynzpan. Their son, Herschel, reacted by carrying out an assassination attempt on an official at the German embassy in Paris on 7th November 1938, who died two days later. His death was used by the Nazi leadership as an excuse for the November pogrom.

The November pogrom

In the night of the 9th to 10th November 1938 the Nazi leadership ordered their people to terrorise the Jews. Both synagogues in Essen – in the city centre and Steele – were set on fire, along with the Jewish Young People's home in Saarbrückerstraße and the Villa Samson. Jewish businesses and property were plundered and destroyed.

Jews in Essen were insulted, assaulted and humiliated. Jewish men between the ages of 16 and 55 were carried off to the concentration camp in Dachau. Scarred by their experiences in the camp most of them only managed to return weeks or months later.

After the November Pogrom

The November pogrom was followed by even harsher humiliation, social exclusion and repression. Jews were sentenced to pay an atonement fee in the form of a "contribution" whose total amounted to around a billion Reich marks. Any remaining Jews were banned from running their own businesses or holding leading positions in society.

They were forced to set up a "Reich Union of Jews" in Germany, to which the Essen community was also subordinate. Hence the chair of the community was ordered to be an intermediary in communicating the regulations of the state. The community's institutions were confiscated and put to new usages. The kindergarten in Peterstraße was turned into a police station, and the old people's home in the Rosenau was converted into a convalescent centre for the Nazi Women's organisation. The Georg Hirschland villa was declared a guest house for the leaders of the regional administration (Gauleitung).

After the synagogue on Steeler Straße was pillaged, the community was forced to set up stopgap accommodation at 22 Hindenburgstraße.

During the Second World War the Nazis began to drive the remaining Jews in Essen from their houses and pool them in so-called "Jews Houses" in the city centre and suburbs.

In spring 1942 most of the Jews still living in Essen were ordered to move to a camp ("Am Holbeckshof"), sited on the grounds of a disused coal mine in the suburb of Steele. The camp was fenced off and guarded, but the internees were allowed to leave it by day. Young people who were still able to work had to undertake forced labour, amongst others. Each of the barracks in the camp consisted of several small rooms and a fireplace. Common rooms, prayer rooms and classrooms were constructed under extremely harsh conditions.

The Shoah
Deportations from Essen began on the 27th October 1941. On that day 261 persons were taken to the ghetto in Lódz. There were nine transports between 1941 and 1943. They took people to ghettos and camps like Lódz, Minsk, Riga and Izbica, all of which were transfer points on the way to the annihilation camps. In 1943 one transport went directly to Auschwitz. The total number of persons deported from Essen was around 1,200. Almost all of them were murdered.

The post-war community
A small community of Jews came together in May 1945. In 1946 it comprised 150 members, mainly survivors from the annihilation camps, amongst whom were a few Jews who had previously lived in Essen. From 1947/48 onwards the community used rooms in the former Rabbi's house as its synagogue, common room and office. In 1959 using the proceeds from the sale of the synagogue building, it built a new synagogue in the Ruhrallee where the Jewish Young People's Home had stood before the 1938 November pogrom. As a result of aging and emigration Jewish life in Essen declined constantly until 1989.

Statistics drawn up by Sergio della Pergola, The Hebrew University of Jerusalem (from the American Jewish Yearbook, 2007, p. 596)
Israel 5,500,000
USA 5,300,000
France 490,000
Canada 374,000
United Kingdom 274,000
Russia 221,000
Argentina 184,000
Germany 120,000
Australia 104,000
Brazil 96,200
Ukraine 79,000
Hungary 49,000
Belgium 30,500

After 1990 a wave of immigration from the former Soviet Union began. Today the Jewish community has 930 members and is part of the Federal Association of Jewish Communities in North Rhine, with its headquarters in Düsseldorf. This in turn belongs to the Central Council of Jews in Germany. Today 110,000 Jews are members of the communities in the Central Council. Since the 1980s the Hasidic Lubavitch movement has been building up structures to try to win over secular Jews to an ultra-orthodox way of life. In the 1990s further liberal and conservative groups were set up. In NRW there are liberal groupings in Cologne, Unna and Oberhausen. All in all today (2016) there are 30,000 Jews living in North-Rhine Westphalia and 110,000 members of the community in Germany. It is not known how many persons are not officially registered as Jews.

Jewish Displaced Persons put a Sukkah
in the destroyed synagogue in about 1948:
A demonstration of Jewish survival?
A call for restitution to Jewish owners?

The current Jewish Community has a lot of
members from Russia and Ukraina

Old Synagogue Essen – House of Jewish Culture

The VIP gallery shows the importance of Jews in modern culture:
Two glimpses, one of Hans Rosenthal (1925–1987) a famous showmaster
in German television in the 1960s and 1970s and the other
of Winona Ryder (1971–), an actress.

Gallery of well-known persons
In the north stairway (and the staircase to the section on the *History of the Jewish Community in Essen*)

This installation shows Jews as leading lights in modern cultural life and life styles. Certain personalities are publicly known to be Jews, others not at all or only to few persons.

1. Allan, Woody (Konigsberg) (1935–), director and actor
2. Arendt, Hannah (1906–1975), scholar of politics
3. Bacall, Lauren (1924–2014), actor
4. Balder, Hugo Egon (1950–), TV show master and producer
5. Bensemann, Walther (1873–1934), founder of the football magazine "kicker" and co-founder of the German Football Association
6. Broder, Henryk M. (1946–), journalist
7. Brooks, Mel (1926–), actor and director

8. Bubis, Ignaz (1927–1999), businessman and President of the Central Council of Jews in Germany
9. Chagall, Marc (1887–1985), artist
10. Cohen, Sacha Baron (1971–), comedian and actor
11. De Vito, Danny (1944–), actor and director
12. Degen, Michael (1932–), actor
13. Douglas, Kirk (Issur Danielowitsch Demsky) (1916–), actor
14. Dylan, Bob (Robert Allen Zimmerman) (1941–), musician
15. Einstein, Albert (1879–1955), physicist, winner of the Nobel prize in 1921
16. Falk, Peter (1927–2011), actor and film producer
17. Frank, Anne (1929–1945), school student and diarist
18. Geller, Uri (1946–), magician
19. Gershwin, George (1898–1937), composer and pianist
20. Giordano, Ralph (1923–2014), journalist and essayist
21. Haza, Ofra (1957–2000), singer Yemenite-Jewish music
22. Hoffman, Dustin (1937–), actor
23. Kafka, Franz (1883–1924), writer
24. Kasparov, Garry (1963–), world chess champion and politician
25. Kishon, Efrajim (Ferenc Hoffmann) (1924–2005), Israeli satirist
26. Kissinger, Henry (Alfred Heinz) (1923–), American politician, 1973–1977 US Foreign Minister, winner of the Nobel Peace Prize
27. Lauder, Estée (1906–2004), cosmetics businesswoman
28. Lavi, Daliah (1942–), singer and actor
29. Luxemburg, Rosa (1871–1919), politician and representative of the working-class movement. Murdered in 1919
30. Matthau, Walter (1920–2000), actor
31. Newman, Paul Leonard (1925-2008), actor and director, Oscar winner
32. Nimoy, Leonard (1931–2015), actor and director
33. Nini, Achinoam (1969–), Israeli singer of Yemenite-Jewish origin
34. Palmer, Lilli (1914–1986), actor and author
35. Peres, Shimon (Szymon Perski) (1923–), politician, Minister President of Israel 1984–1986, 1994/95, President of Israel 2007-2014
36. Portman, Nathalie (1981–), actor
37. Rabin, Yitzhak (1922–1995), politician, Minister President of Israel 1974–1977, 1992–1995, winner of the Nobel prize 1994
38. Refaeli, Bar (1985–), model
39. Reich-Ranicki, Marcel (1920–2010), literary critic
40. Richter, Ilja (1952–), actor and TV compère
41. Rosenthal, Hans (1925–1987), entertainer and member of the directorate of the Central Council of Jews in Germany
42. Ryder, Winona (1971–), actor
43. Sandler, Adam (1966–), actor
44. Spielberg, Steven (1946–), director and producer
45. Stiller, Ben (1965–), actor and screenwriter
46. Strauss, Levi (Löb) (1829–1902), industrialist and marketer of blue jeans. Originally from Buttenheim in Franconia. Emigrated to the USA in 1847
47. Wiesenthal, Simon (1908–2005), architect and publicist
48. Winehouse, Amy (1983–2011), singer and songwriter
49. Wolffsohn, Michael (1947–), historian

The authors

Edna Brocke
Studies in Political Science, English Language and Literature and Jewish Studies at the Hebrew University of Jerusalem. She was director of the Old Synagogue between 1988 und 2011.

Lothar Jeromin
Architect in the Association of German Architects (BDA). He supervised the refurbishing between 2006 and 2010. He owns an architecture and planning office in Essen-Bredeney.

Uri R. Kaufmann
Studies of General and Jewish History at the Hebrew University of Jerusalem, Ph.D. at Zurich University, research on Social History of Jews in Central Europe, director of the Old Synagogue since September 2011.

Dorothee Rauhut
Studies of the History of Art in Braunschweig and Berlin. She has been working as guide in the Old Synagogue since 2005, also in the Ruhr Museum and the city archives of Essen.

Peter Schwiderowski
Ph.D. in Social Scienes and History, between 1997 and 2013 researcher and vice-director of the Old Synagogue. Since 2013 he works for the city archive of Essen.

Martina Strehlen
M. A. in Jewish Studies, Library Sciences and Islam in Cologne, Jerusalem and Berlin. She works as head of the collections, researcher and vice director of the Old Synagogue since 2004.

The permanent exhibition

Concept of the permanent exhibition:
Edna Brocke, Peter Schwiderowski, Martina Strehlen

Jewish Way of Life:
Agentur jüdische Kulturvermittlung Esther Graf, Manja Altenburg, Heidelberg/Mannheim

Steering team:
Andreas Bomheuer, Petra Beckers, Kurt Busch, Rainer Dehne, Barbara Heine, Michael Imberg, Rolf Nienaber, Henning Osthues-Albrecht, Andrea Richter, Uwe Theisen, Kerstin Uredat, Mathias Wellekötter

Project manager of reconstruction:
Stephanie Frevel, Helge Seidel

Art director, interior architecture and scenography:
Jürg Steiner BDA mit Alexander Becker, Andreas Froncala, Olaf Mehl, Philip Schröder, Colin Steiner, Kolja Thomas, Cüneyt Yurdakul

IT-work:
LVR Zentrum für Medien und Bildung, Düsseldorf, Tom Lovens, Angela Giebmeyer

Head of reconstruction work:
Lothar Jeromin BDA

Design of illumination:
Dinnebier-Licht GmbH, Wuppertal

Technicall matters:
Ingenieurbüro Paulus GmbH, Essen

Landscaping:
wpb Landschaftsarchitekten, Bochum

Sponsors:
Ministry for Construction and Traffic of the state of North Rhine-Westphalia, Düsseldorf
Deichmann Stiftung, Essen
Landschaftsverband Rheinland, Köln
Stiftung Alte Synagoge Essen
Sparkasse Essen
Stadtwerke Essen AG
NRW-Stiftung, Düsseldorf
Allbau AG, Essen
Wolff Gruppe Holding GmbH, Essen
Deutsche Bank, Essen
Anneliese Brost-Stiftung Essen
Alfred und Cläre Pott Stiftung, Essen
Elektro Decker, Essen

Picture credits

Beit Tfila-Project, PD Dr.-Ing. habil. Ulrich Knufinke, University of Braunschweig, p. 61 (left)

City of Essen, Alte Synagoge, collection/archive p. 11, 17, 18, 19, 22, 23 (both), 29, 83 (left), 85, 87, 110, 145, 146 (left und right), 148, 149 (bottom), 156 (both), 165, 170, 177 (top), 185, 189 (bottom), 195 (pencil drawing), 197, 203 (top)
City of Essen, Brigitte Giesen, p. 117, 156, 169 (left), 192 (both), 196
City of Essen, Hans Peter Prengel, photo editing, p. 27, 28
City of Essen, Harald Thiet, p. 189 (top)
City of Essen, city archives, p. 59 (file of the house)

City of Wittlich, cultural affairs department, Werner Pelm, p. 66 bottom left

Förderkreis Görlitzer Synagoge, Jördis Heizmann, p. 68 (bottom right)

Hammer-Schenk, Harold: Synagogen in Deutschland. Geschichte einer Baugattung im 19. und 20. Jahrhundert, part II, Hamburg 1981, p. 61 (right, there illustration no. 107), 63 (there illustration no. 4), 64 (there illustration no. 201, 202, 151), p. 66f. (all except Wittlich and Görlitz, there illustration no. 390, 405, 411, 418, 422, 428f., 440, 445, 448), 68 (there illustration no. 409, 410, 446, not Görlitz), 70 (there illustration no. 443, 447)

Jeromin, Lothar, Essen, p. 83 (right), 98f., 102, 105 (both), 106 (all 3), 111 (drawing), 113, 117

Lukas, Georg, Essen, p. 204, 21, 129 (both), 141 (both), 142, 146 (left), 149 (top), 150 (both), 152f., 156 (both), 158–161, 163f., 166, 167f., 169 (right), 176, 177 (bottom), 179, 181 (both), 184, 192 (bottom), 195 (both paintings), 196, 203 (bottom), 204 (all 3)

Stiftung Ruhr Museum, photo archive, p. 8, 14f., 173

Uchrin, Stefan, Wuppertal, p. 146

Unichor Essen, p. 25

Valerius, Evelyn, Essen, p. 30